COUPLES &MONEY

*Cracking the code to ending
the #1 conflict in marriage*

COUPLES & MONEY

Cracking the code to ending the #1 conflict in marriage

JACKIE BLACK, PHD

Outskirts Press, Inc.
Denver, Colorado

Notice:

This book is intended as a reference only; to educate, inform and entertain. It should not be used as the ultimate source of information about money and marriage. It is designed to give information with regard to the subject matter covered, and the information provided is designed to help you make informed decisions about marriage and money. It is not intended to be a substitute for individual, marital, or family therapy, or for legal, financial, accounting or other professional advice or services. It is sold with the understanding that the publisher and author are not engaged in rendering individual, marital or family therapy, or legal, financial, accounting or other professional advice. If marital, legal, financial, accounting advice or other expert advice is required; the services of a competent professional should be sought.

Names and identifying details in the personal stories have been changed to ensure confidentiality. The opinions expressed in this manuscript are solely the opinions of the author and do not represent the opinions or thoughts of the publisher. The author has represented and warranted full ownership and/or legal right to publish all the materials in this book.

Couples and Money: Cracking the code to ending the #1 conflict in marriage
All Rights Reserved.
Copyright © 2010 Jackie Black, Ph.D.
v2.0

Cover Design: Sandra Selle-Rodriguez, Graphics and Fine Art; selle-rodriguez.com

This book may not be reproduced, transmitted, or stored in whole or in part by any means, including graphic, electronic, or mechanical without the express written consent of the publisher except in the case of brief quotations embodied in critical articles and reviews.

Outskirts Press, Inc.
http://www.outskirtspress.com

ISBN: 978-1-4327-5060-2

Library of Congress Control Number: 2010933548

Outskirts Press and the "OP" logo are trademarks belonging to Outskirts Press, Inc.

PRINTED IN THE UNITED STATES OF AMERICA

AUTHOR DEDICATION

This book is dedicated to the loving memory of my grandfather, Lewis D. Ross.

When I was growing up my grandfather and I used to sit together after breakfast. He would read the Wall Street Journal and I would read my Nancy Drew books. I would wait patiently for the moment that he would look up and ask me if I wanted to take a look at the stock market page with him. I would sit as close to him as I could, and together we would look up and down and across the columns of tiny numbers and funny symbols. He would tell me wonderful stories about the companies, their products and services, and the men who ran them.

We would sit there, for what seemed like hours, talking about his beliefs and experiences about earning, spending, saving and investing money. I am honored to have the opportunity to share my thoughts and ideas about money that have deep roots in my relationship with my beloved grandfather.

WORDS OF PRAISE FOR COUPLES AND MONEY
Cracking the code to ending the #1 conflict in marriage

"Unfortunately, Dr. Jackie Black's book *Couples and Money* does not come at the perfect time. That perfect time would have been several years ago before excessive debt and spending chased the nation and many of its consumers to the economic brink. Still, as those consumers seek to rebuild their lives and financial ideas, a good place to start would be Dr. Black's book.

In the book, Dr. Black does an extraordinary job of getting to the root basis and psychology that shape our views about money and spending. While Americans are prone to self and external evaluation about a host of issues that face our lives, rarely do we confront the basic values of one of the most dominant influences in our culture, which is money.

I would recommend this book not only for the couples it is designed to teach and help, but for all that are seeking to gain a financial ownership of their lives and a positive energy from money and its influences."

Andrew Montgomery
Chairman and Chief Executive Officer
Western Community Bancshares, Inc.

"*Couples and Money* by Dr. Jackie Black presents practical solutions for resolving money conflicts faced by those in relationships. Dr. Jackie's suggestion to view finances as a family business coupled with techniques for communicating effectively about money make this book a valuable resource."

Joan Sotkin
Author of *Build Your Money Muscles*

ix

"*Couples and Money* is probably the best book on the topic of how money can either make or break a marriage or life partnership that I have ever read. I realized about half-way through the book that my husband and I 'talk around' and argue about money at least 5 times a week (if not daily) and that other smaller arguments about raising children, taking vacations or dining out are rooted in the topic of money. We have always worked hard, saved money, invested well and as a result, we have very little debt, but these tiny arguments are just not necessary...they are all about 'what if this happens,' and they are grounded in things that simply are not true. As a result of reading *Couples and Money,* my husband and I had our first strategic discussion about our finances, and we were both laughing about how our beliefs go way back to how our fathers both handled money (which Dr. Jackie addresses in the book). We had a huge breakthrough simply talking about this one issue, and we have made the decision that it is time to downsize our home and start using weekly 'cash only' allowances. I feel so relieved that we have a plan! This book is a must read for all married couples and for any couples who are dating and considering marriage. Just go ahead and pick up 3 copies and give them to your family members as a gift...they will thank you forever!"

Bea Fields
Author of *Millennial Leaders and EDGE! A Leadership Story*

"While money can't buy you love, fighting over it can bankrupt your marriage–particularly, if you or your partner have some of the symptoms of impulsivity, disorganization and forgetfulness associated with ADD/ADHD. Dr. Jackie's strategies in *Couples & Money* for building the **Family Business** will be especially helpful for partners with ADD/ADHD who are committed to achieving financial fitness in their marriage."

Shane K. Perrault, Ph.D.
ADHD Performance Clinic

"Reading Dr. Jackie's book, *Couples and Money*, made me reflect on the thirty-four years that I have been married and more particularly, on the early years of our marriage. During the early years, the common cause of many a heated argument centered around financial matters. I know that the majority of couples starting out in life face financially-related pressures, and *Couples and Money* goes a long way to address how couples can best face these pressures and preserve their marriage. I regret that Dr. Jackie's book was not available in the early years of my marriage. It is essential that all couples starting out read this book and practice the sound principles set forth in it. I have advised my two daughters who have recently married, to buy a copy of Dr. Jackie's book and take heed of the no-nonsense, reliable information in it! Dr. Jackie's book *Couples and Money* is a practical guide for partners to address one of the major hurdles they will have to overcome in their marriage–and that is the sound, practical management of their financial affairs."

Tim Davidson
Chairman, WA Davidson Financial Services (Pty) Ltd.
Johannesburg, South Africa

"This book provides easy-to-understand guidelines and fundamentals on how to successfully blend both love and money. Dr. Jackie provides solid, straightforward insight on everything from understanding the psychology of money to effectively communicating about an extremely stressful and volatile topic with your partner in a way that creates more calm and ease. This is a book that you can reference time and again as different financial/ relationship issues arise in your life to support you in getting back on track!"

Leslie Cunningham
Financial Dating* Expert and Money coach

"*Couples and Money* is the perfect guide to help you reconcile romance and finance. If you care about your relationship, Dr. Jackie's book is an essential addition to your home library!

Dr. Jackie has created an intimate look at the relationship we have with money and how finances affect our relationships with a spouse. There is nobody better suited for this work than Dr. Jackie Black and *Couples and Money* is a powerful reflection of her warmth, expertise and sensitive but rational approach to love and money.

Dr. Jackie helps the reader develop a synergy between romance and finance that will help keep your relationship solid. She lays out a clear and understandable plan reinforced with accessible stories and examples from her work as one of the world's leading relationship experts. She includes a series of clear exercises that transform the odious discussion of money to an enjoyable and productive activity for you and your partner!

You may want to change old habits, or you may be just starting out as a couple. Dr. Jackie's book may save your relationship or help you create a long, successful and happy life with the person you love!"

Jim Bouchard
Speaker, Black Belt Mindset Master &
Author of *Think Like a Black Belt*

"Smart Book! It's one of those books that after you read it once, you can pick it up anytime and use it as a reference for great money tips. The thought provoking questions will create a better money relationship between you and your partner. You can't lose with this one!"

Kary Shafer
Owner, Money Awareness

"Dr. Jackie Black has given every couple the complete tools they need to handle one of the hardest issues we all have to deal with in a relationship...money. In *Couples and Money*, Dr. Black doesn't just discuss the issues, she provides real solutions that are fun and easy to apply. Money is a difficult subject for most couples to talk about, but with this indispensable guide, the topic of money never again has to be something to avoid. Dr. Black creates a relaxing and hands on environment to ultimately remove all the issues that can cause problems in a relationship around money. What a gift! Everyone should have this valuable resource at their fingertips."

Anne Leedom
Founder, Parentingbookmark.com

"Anyone who's ever longed for peace and harmony about financial issues in their relationship can benefit from the down-to-earth knowledge in this book. This is an easy-read with a wealth of solid, user-friendly information!"

Valerie Israel, DO, CC
Health and Wellness Coach

TABLE OF CONTENTS

AUTHOR DEDICATION vii

WORDS OF PRAISE ix

FOREWORD xxi

ACKNOWLEDGEMENTS xxiii

INTRODUCTION xxv

Chapter 1
REALIZE CONFLICTS BY RECOGNIZING HOW YOUR PAST INFLUENCES YOUR FINANCIAL PRESENT AND FUTURE.... 1
Your Beliefs about Money 3
Your Values Related to Money 3
Your Attitudes about Money..5
Your Behaviors Related to Money 5
Successfully Challenge and Change Your Early Beliefs about Money....6
Successfully Challenge and Change Your Values about Money.............8
Successfully Challenge and Change Your Attitudes about Money..........9
Successfully Challenge and Change Your Behaviors Related to Money 10
Make Sustainable Changes in Everyday Money Decisions 11

Chapter 2
UNDERSTAND YOUR MONEY PSYCHOLOGY AND DIFFERENCES THAT CAUSE CONFLICT 15
The Psychology of Money 16
Money Scripts 17
Prosperity Thinking or Abundance Scripting 17
Poverty Thinking or Scarcity Scripting 18
Money is Neutral...19
Hoarders...20
Under-Spenders 20
Spenders or Amassers 21
Over-Spenders 21

Chapter 3
AVOID CONFLICT BY UNDERSTANDING THE ENERGY OF MONEY 25
You Give Money Its Energy! 26
Explore Common Clichés and Build New Beliefs about Money 27

Change False Beliefs and Assumptions about Money 29
Abundance and Prosperity Are an Inside Job! 33
Intentional Decisions and Choices Related to Money 34

Chapter 4
ALL ABOUT DEBT—ESCAPE THE CONFLICT 37
Is Debt Weakening Your Financial Fitness? 37
Tell the Truth About Your Money—Intentionally and Regularly! 38
Keeping Spending in Check 39
Credit Cards 40
Using Debt to Pay Off Debt and Spiraling Debt................................40
Taking Out Loans..41
Emergency Fund 42
Gambling 42

Chapter 5
VALUES, ATTITUDES, BELIEFS AND HABITS RELATED TO MANAGING MONEY, BUILDING WEALTH AND PREVENTING CONFLICT 47
Your Values..47
Needs and Values 49
Your Beliefs and Attitudes...49
Your Habits 51
Earning Your Money 52
Spending Your Money 53
Accounting for Your Money..54
Saving Your Money..56
Investing and Contributing Your Money...57
Investing Your Money 57
Contributing Your Money 58
Building Wealth for Your Future...60

Chapter 6
WAKE UP! YOU AND YOUR PARTNER CAN END MONEY CONFLICTS TOGETHER! 63
Wake Up and Be a Conscious Partner! 63
Become Emotionally Intelligent in Your Relationship! 64
Must-Have Agreements in Your Conscious Relationship 64
Be Aware of What Lies Inside You That Can Threaten Your Love
Connection 65
Relationship Issues Are Opportunities for Your Personal Growth 66
Communication Break Downs 66
Learn and Practice Three Main Listening Skills 67
The Four Basic Commitments of Conscious Couples............................68
Legitimate Needs and Wants 68

Chapter 7
BUILD THE FAMILY BUSINESS AND HEAD OFF CONFLICTS
BEFORE THEY START 71
Strategies When One Partner Earns All or Most of the Money 72
Strategies When Both Partners Earn Money................................72
Schedule Regular Money Conversations 74
Speak with Each Other Respectfully and Responsibly during Money
Conversations 75
Support Each Other to Resolve Disagreements about Money..............75
Your Responsibilities in Your *Family Business* 76
Think of Your Budget as Your Spending Plan.......................................77
Set Joint Savings and Retirement Goals..78
Set Joint Investing Goals and Commit to Wealth-Building Behaviors ...78
Do Not Commit Financial Infidelity and Threaten the Integrity of the
Family Business 79
Teach Your Children about Sound Money Management 80

Chapter 8
YOUR FINANCIAL VISION AND GOALS ARE KEY TO
ENDING MONEY CONFLICTS FROM THIS DAY FORWARD 83
Vision and Goals: A Definition 83
My Vision of My Ideal Life..84
My Vision for My Ideal Life, Which Includes My Partner 85
My Partner's Vision of His/Her Ideal Life...86
Our Vision for Our Life Together...86
Our Vision for Our Financial Life 87
Our Short-Term Goals 91
Our Mid-Term Goals 92
Our Long-Term Goals..92
Your Commitments That Support and Forward Your Financial Vision ..93

Chapter 9
MASTERING ESSENTIAL RELATIONSHIP SUCCESS SKILLS
FOR EFFECTIVE COMMUNICATION MEANS RESOLVING
CONFLICTS WITH ONE VOICE.. 95
Six Skills for Effectively Resolving Conflicts about Money 96
Three Mistakes Couples Make When It Comes to Resolving Conflicts
about Money...96
Know What Affects Your Ability to Resolve Conflicts about Money! 97
Five Steps to Problem-Solve Issues about Money...............................98
Five Rules of Engagement to Effectively Communicate about Money ..99
    Rule #1: Get Yourself Grounded and in the Right Mind-set 99
    Rule #2: Self-Esteem Reminder Checklist 100
    Rule #3: Always Engage In a Conversation From The "I"
    Position 100

Rule #4: Assess Your Readiness and Your Partner's Readiness to Communicate Effectively 101
Rule #5: Speak for the Sole Purpose of Being Known.................102

Chapter 10
CRAFT ELEGANT AGREEMENTS AND END MONEY CONFLICTS FOREVER! 103
The Purpose of an Elegant Agreement 103
Schedule an Intentional Conversation and Co-Create an Elegant Agreement..103
Before You Create an Elegant Agreement..104
Dr. Jackie's 15-Step Process to Create an Elegant Agreement 104
Attitudes, Beliefs and Judgments Can Skew the Process.................106

Chapter 11
GRATITUDE STOPS CONFLICT ONCE AND FOR ALL........ 109
Appreciating and Being Grateful...109
Gratitude is NOT Putting on Rose-Colored Glasses 109
Gratitude is a Deliberate, Intentional Behavior 111
Begin YOUR Practice of Gratitude 112
Three True Stories... 113
Why and How to Show Your Appreciation 113
Showing Others Appreciation is One Side of the Coin 115
Create a Gratitude Journal 115
Commit to Making Changes Specifically Related to Earning, Spending, Accounting for, Saving, and Investing Money Consciously and with Purpose 117

Chapter 12
AVOID THE NEGATIVE IMPACT OF ADHD ON YOU AND YOUR FAMILY BUSINESS... 119
Your Problem Areas with Money 119
Your Vision for Your Life and Your *Family Business* 121
Your Goals and Your *Family Business* 121
Shop 'Till You Drop 123
Reach Out and Find Support..124

EPILOGUE 125

APPENDIX 129
Worksheet 1— *My Vision of My Ideal Life*....................................130
Worksheet 2a— *My Vision for My Ideal Life, Which Includes My Partner* 132
Worksheet 2b— *My Vision for My Ideal Life, Which Includes My Partner* 135
Worksheet 3a— *My Partner's Vision of His/Her Ideal Life* 136

Worksheet 3b— *My Partner's Vision of His/Her Ideal Life Including Me* 139

Worksheet 3c— *My Partner's Vision of His/Her Ideal Life Including Me* 142

Worksheet 4— *Our Vision of Our Life Together* 143

Worksheet 5— *Our Vision of Our Financial Life* 147

Worksheet 6a—*Our Short-term Goals--Personal Goal-Setting Abilities* 148

Worksheet 6b— *Our Short-term Goals—Setting the Goals* 150

Worksheet 7a— *Our Mid-term Goals—Personal Goal-Setting Abilities* 153

Worksheet 7b— *Our Mid-term Goals—Setting the Goals* 155

Worksheet 8a— *Our Long-term Goals—Personal Goal-Setting Abilities* 158

Worksheet 8b— *Our Long-term Goals—Setting the Goals* 160

Worksheet 9— *Our Commitments that will Make Our Financial Vision a Reality* 163

Worksheet 10— *Your Final Thoughts* 164

GLOSSARY OF TERMS 167

ABOUT THE AUTHOR 173

A SNEAK PREVIEW OF DR. JACKIE'S NEXT BOOK.......... 177

FOREWORD

After rewarding, successful careers in our respective fields, Dr. Jackie's path and mine paralleled in making a full transition to Professional Coaching. Those paths intersected when we were both invited to join the Faculty of Coach Training Alliance at about the same time.

At our Faculty meetings, I have listened to her progress notes with awe: invitations to present workshops to prestigious groups on different continents; innovative endeavors in teaching and coaching about relationships and groups. I see her leveraged impact as a prolific author. She is one of those extraordinary people for whom the word "brilliant" must have been invented.

Dr. Jackie has written a book that will interest you only in two situations: if you are in a relationship with another human being; and if you plan to use money at any time for the rest of your life.

Successful, lasting relationships that incorporate money, harmony, and prosperity do not just happen. In fact, they don't "just happen" to the extent that post-divorce surveys indicate that more than 90% of couples cite money problems as a turning point in their relationship. The greatest challenge in coaching couples is how to mentor understanding and guide change in their money relationship.

Every relationship combines two individual stories into one co-authored new story. Each party in a relationship brings unspoken assumptions and implicit contracts to the relationship. Couples co-create a money story that they often do not know how to tell to themselves, in order to be able to change.

When you feel with one part of your brain and plan with another, you need a map. When two people come together, each has a unique relationship with money, and they need a system to bridge to a common ground.

Co-creating a mutually satisfying and fulfilling money relationship challenges every couple. The new co-authored story will devise its own communication, behaviors, metaphors, patterns, goals, and visions.

As both cartographer and guide (and it's a very rare writer who can skillfully weave both together). Dr. Jackie mentors couples to understand their individual relationships with money in order to create a unified money story together. She provides them with the tools, methods, and principles to create their own blueprint for a successful money relationship. This system is a users' manual for couples.

There's a secret hiding in the open: When you practice these success skills, all the aspects of your relationship that money symbolizes will also benefit.

So, you're in for a treat with this book. And get ready to work. You are beginning an endeavor to create understanding and harmony in your relationship with money. Be prepared for two experiences to transcend that mission. Dr. Jackie will catalyze your journey to embrace wealth, as well as to evolve your relationship with each other.

David Krueger, M.D.
CEO, MentorPath
Author, *The Secret Language of Money*

ACKNOWLEDGEMENTS

I am grateful to the small army of people who were supportive, encouraging and helpful in many ways: including reading and commenting on parts of drafts, and improving this book with every comment, question and criticism they offered; giving examples from their own personal experiences; and discussing ideas with me.

I deeply appreciate the kind and generous endorsements I have received from other authors, friends and colleagues.

I thank Vicki Besemer for everything you do. You are the rudder to my ship, the implementer of my visions. Without you, I could not do the work I am called to do or realize my professional goals. Thank you for your commitment to excellence in all that we do and for your eternal optimism and permission to vent when the going gets tough.

My heartfelt thanks to Barbara Elion–a masterful editor! Your exacting, comprehensive and elegant copy-editing has turned my manuscript into "the best possible book."

My sincere thanks to Maria Kutscher, CFA, CFP, Vice President, Wealth Management, American Century Investments. I thank you so much for sharing with me your knowledge, thoughts and experiences of couples building wealth. Your stories validated my experience with couples and spurred me on in the very early writing of this book.

My appreciation to Suzanne Zemelman Gellman, M.S., J.D., Consumer Economics Specialist at the University of Missouri

xxiii

Extension. I thoroughly enjoyed our conversations and appreciate you sharing your knowledge and wisdom about couples and money.

Thank you to Shane K. Perrault, Ph.D., founder of ADHD Performance Counseling, for so generously sharing your vast knowledge about ADHD in adults and the specific issues related to money, and for all the rich stories you told me that deeply informed my understanding of ADHD and money.

I am grateful to my clients. My deepest gratitude is extended to you for allowing me to be present with you on your journey to being your best and most brilliant, passionate Self in the presence of each other and to being a most conscious and emotionally intelligent partner in your relationship. You are all my most influential teachers and mentors.

INTRODUCTION

Managing your money with your partner and building wealth are basic fundamental requirements of being a healthy, committed couple.

Congratulations! Buying this book is the first step on the road to take back control and ownership of your financial life.

As with so many other essential relationship success skills, you don't realize, while building a life together as partners, that the tried and true business principles that successful business people have depended on for decades are the same principles that will support you in talking about money, in making decisions about money, and in enabling you to make your dreams come true.

You can read this book from cover to cover in several hours or less. Then I suggest you read it again, answering the questions in detail that are posed in the course of each chapter, and completing the Worksheets in Chapter 8 and at the very end of the book.

The book is written with the intention that it is read chapter by chapter. This will help you to make sense out of the information as well as provide the stimulus for you to use what you have learned to make your life and your financial life better. If you skip around, the material may be misunderstood and may be more difficult to implement.

By the time you finish this book, you will be able to completely change your personal relationship with money, and to transform money issues in your marriage! If you have some solid values, beliefs, attitudes and habits related to money and money matters in your marriage that are

xxv

working for you, use the skills and tools recommended to strengthen any financial weak spots that are limiting you.

The information in this book will help you recognize where you are, how you got here, where you want to go and how to get there!

COUPLES AND MONEY: Cracking the code to ending the #1 conflict in marriage includes 12 chapters. In each chapter I have included important questions to ask yourself: sometimes a story about a couple, their issues and how they were able to solve their problems using the skills discussed and the recommendations made in that chapter. I have written a brief summary for every chapter so that you know how this book will fortify your marriage.

Chapter 1:

Chapter 1 is a full discussion that will help you recognize how your past has deeply affected and continues to influence your financial present and future.

At the end of this chapter you will understand what your values, beliefs, attitudes and behaviors are as they relate to money; and you'll have powerful ways to challenge them and change them so they work better for you in your life today and tomorrow.

Chapter 2:

In Chapter 2, we'll explore the whole idea surrounding money psychology. You'll learn about your own money psychology, which will be important when you and your partner begin to "Build Your *Family Business*" in Chapter 7.

xxvi

You will see yourself and your partner walking through the pages of this chapter. Whether your money psychology is based in prosperity thinking or scarcity thinking, no worries! By the time you get through Chapter 12 you will have successfully and forever changed your relationship with money.

Chapter 3:

Do you know that money is energy? Chapter 3 will focus on how YOU give money energy; and help you identify your false beliefs, assumptions and myths about money so you can change the ideas that limit you and create beliefs that will support you to become financially fit!

Money freedom requires that your thoughts, feelings, actions and beliefs about money match! That is, when what you do, think, and say all match each other. At the end of Chapter 3 you'll have an excellent grasp of the notion that you'll never be free if you say that you have more than enough money–and then behave (and think) as though you don't, and you'll never be free if you think you don't have enough money; and then act as though you do and say you do.

Chapter 4:

Chapter 4 might take you by surprise when we unwrap the whole area of debt and incurring debt with no holds barred! We'll explore the naked truth without excuses or distractions.

Debt isn't something that just happens to you. Your spending habits lead you directly into debt. By the end of Chapter 4, I predict that you will be anxious to start shifting your consciousness from *debt-consciousness* to *wealth-building*

xxvii

consciousness, and you'll be actively looking to make this a top priority!

Chapter 5:

As we work through Chapter 5, it might be the first time in your life that you will actually explore your values, attitudes, beliefs and habits related to earning, spending, saving, investing/contributing money, and building wealth; and we'll do this in very rich detail.

When you get to the end of Chapter 5 you will have so much rich, powerful information about yourself that you will, more than likely, begin using it immediately. My clients who get to this point are thrilled to have this massive amount of personal information and, at the same time, are furious that they never got this information anywhere before.

Chapter 6:

Even though you are a couple, your participation as an individual, and your partner's participation as an individual, impacts, affects and influences all the choices and decisions you make, or don't make, as a couple. In Chapter 6 we are going to focus on YOU and your obligations and responsibilities as an emotionally intelligent partner in a conscious relationship!

Being an emotionally intelligent person and co-creating a conscious relationship with another emotionally intelligent person seems like a simple concept, doesn't it? Unfortunately, people sometimes get through their whole lives without being introduced to these concepts and skills. Now that you have been, you cannot go back to being unconscious in your life or in your relationship.

Chapter 7:

There isn't one right way for you to manage your money and build wealth. In Chapter 7 we'll explore the nature and structure of the strategies you can use to build and grow your *Family Business*. First, we'll take a look at the six most common ways to manage your money, and then at a process that will support you to resolve disagreements about money.

Chapter 7 will also explore the idea of setting up regular couple **Money Conversations** to decide who is going to be responsible for doing what in your *Family Business*. You'll learn how to develop a spending plan; savings and retirement goals; commitments to wealth-building behaviors; ways to teach your children about sound money management so as to involve them in your *Family Business*, and explore what it means to contribute to something greater than yourself.

Chapter 8:

Chapter 8 is your opportunity to create a blueprint: the *how-to* to go inside yourself and figure out what you want your love life and your financial life to include. I developed sixteen Worksheets to support you as you explore *YOU*; then move on to explore *You + Your Partner* (as two equal adults), and end with a full exploration of your *US*.

Not only can you find the Worksheets in the Appendix at the back of the book, you can also find them online at http://www. crackingthecodebooks.com/couples-money_worksheets.htm. Download them to your computer and print them out as often as you want to.

xxix

You will create your blueprint using specific tools: Visions, which are very detailed ideas of your desired outcome(s) that you create in your imagination, and Goals, which are well-defined outcomes that gives you clarity, direction, motivation, and focus.

At the end of the chapter you and your partner will be able to develop the commitments that you both believe make sense, and that you both can and will honor so as to make your financial visions, hopes and dreams your financial realities!

Chapter 9:

Chapter 9 is a comprehensive discussion of the 'must-have' essential relationship success skills that you and your partner will use over and over in many circumstances throughout your life together. Money is only a microcosm of your life and of your relationship. When you learn, practice and master these skills, you will be able to manage your money better, and co-create your financial fitness to build wealth.

This chapter is divided into two parts. Part One relates to specific relationship success skills; Part Two sets forth the Rules of Engagement so that you, as a couple, will have a safe structure to discuss and resolve emotionally charged issues.

Many years ago, I was delivering a presentation in a school auditorium and the audience was primarily couples. About fifteen minutes into my presentation, a man jumped up and started waving his hand in the air and he was yelling, "Dr. Jackie, Dr. Jackie, please, Dr. Jackie." I stopped talking and walked out from behind the podium and said, "Hello! What is it that you would like to say to me, please?" He said, "I love what you're saying, and I didn't think I would. I agree with everything you're saying, and I didn't think I would. If you can tell me H-O-W to do these things, really give me steps to follow, I would be very happy to do these things in my marriage with my wife!"

This man's words struck me like a ton of bricks. It was in that moment that I realized so clearly that no one was actually teaching relationship skills to couples. We are constantly learning in school; we get special training and education for our jobs and careers, and yet, we are somehow expected to know how to have successful, lasting relationships. Chapter 9 does a very good job of exploring several areas of essential relationship success skills.

Chapter 10:

Once you and your partner have completely discussed an issue and you are ready to make a decision or to take action, you'll want to craft an elegant agreement so each of you will know what the agreement is and who is responsible for the action. Chapter 10 will explore the purpose of an elegant agreement and walk you through the 15-step process to create that agreement.

This process is so easy and makes so much sense that you'll find yourself crafting elegant agreements with everyone involved in your life!

Chapter 11:

There is no limit to what you don't have, and if that is where you put your focus, then your life will inevitably be filled with endless dissatisfaction. Most people focus so heavily on the deficiencies in their lives that they barely perceive the good that counterbalances them. Chapter 11 will show you how to get into the habit of showing appreciation, being grateful and recognizing the multitude of goodies you didn't realize were there until you began your practice of gratitude.

A full discussion of the practice of gratitude and appreciation is generally very eye-opening for men and women alike! It is highly likely that it will make very good sense to you, and you will immediately become interested in beginning your practice of gratitude in some way or another. There is usually one sticking point: Your ability to accept appreciation when others convey their appreciation to YOU can be exceptionally challenging. Watch out for this and remember that practice makes perfect!

Chapter 12:

An important and little discussed connection between Adult ADHD and "money behavior" is the focus of Chapter 12. Managing your *Family Business* is a unique challenge for people with ADHD. There are very good reasons for this. This chapter will connect the dots between some of the common characteristics of ADHD in adults and the essential relationship success skills; and remind you that creating your financial vision and your financial goals is the key to ending money conflicts forever.

More and more experts say ADHD can be a gift rather than a malady.

David Neeleman, CEO of JetBlue Airways, says his ADHD one of his biggest assets. Neelamn credits his ADHD with giving him the creativity that helped him develop an electronic ticketing system and pioneer several discount airlines.

Experts make the case over and over that adults with ADHD are creative, intuitive, tenacious and high-energy. They are successful artists and CEOs. They can think outside of the box and are willing to take risks, which makes them successful entrepreneurs.

Remember, it's how you manage your ADHD or not, that determines whether it's a gift or a curse. Chapter 12 refers back to other chapters in this book and provides the map for adults with ADHD who are consciously learning to build and manage the *Family Business*.

In closing, let me gently remind you that you did not get here all by yourself. But you must get out of here all alone!

Money cannot make you happy, but intentional decisions and choices related to money can provide the means of unlimited good for you and many others in your life.

You will have more than enough money when you believe you will; when you take the appropriate actions that positively express your belief; and when you realize that you can be wealthy no matter how much money you earn, save, spend or invest because you are more than your money, and more than your money can buy.

Henry Ford said it best: *"If money is your hope for independence you will never have it. The only real security that a man will have in this world is a reserve of knowledge, experience, and ability."*

Remember, only YOU can make it happen!

Jackie Black, Ph.D.
Southern California
USA

Chapter 1

REALIZE CONFLICTS BY RECOGNIZING HOW YOUR PAST INFLUENCES YOUR FINANCIAL PRESENT AND FUTURE

The research and anecdotal information is in!

The vast majority of married couples argue over money, making it the major reason couples fight and divorce.

Money disputes and differences are the number one leading cause of tension, conflict, marital dissatisfaction and divorce among contemporary couples.

If you and your partner are like most couples, chances are you've had an argument about money today or yesterday!

Many experts will tell you that you have to learn to talk about money, and learn how to work things out!

Not so! Talking alone won't be enough. There is a ton of research that demonstrates that married couples talk about money several times a week. Then what's the problem, you ask?

The problem is that couples are talking emotionally and reactively rather than strategically and proactively!

What would you say if I told you that your past–how your mother and father handle money and the beliefs they have about money– seriously influenced your early thoughts and behaviors related

1

to money, and continues to influence your current thoughts and behaviors related to money? Would you believe me? Here is a story to illustrate my point.

John and Barb's Story

John and Barb have been married for over five years. They both have careers they love; they are upwardly mobile, and they have no money problems to speak of–meaning they can easily pay their monthly bills and buy what they want when they want something for themselves or each other, for their home, or for friends and family members.

John grew up in a small town and his family always had a hard time making ends meet every month. His father was a loving and responsible husband and father, who always worked hard, but just couldn't seem to get ahead.

John had one older brother and one older sister, and he grew up getting his brother's hand-me-down clothes. At the beginning of each school year, John's mother bought John, and each of his siblings, one pair of shoes for school and one "good" pair of shoes for church and special occasions. Every summer–for as many summers as he could remember–John, his brother and his sister had summer jobs.

John's father used to say, "Money doesn't grow on trees, my boy!" "A penny saved is a penny earned." "Time is money." "Never spend your money before you have it."

Barb's mother and father had a *Family Business* and by most standards were considered to be *well-to-do*. Barb's mother worked with her father in the business and Barb and her sister were frequently over-indulged by their mother as a way to make up for her being away so many hours every day. They frequently went on shopping sprees; each of the girls was given a generous allowance; neither was required or even encouraged to pay for their own clothes or entertainment; and they took a family vacation every summer.

Your Beliefs about Money

Your early life experiences serve to deeply inform your beliefs about who you are, how the world works, and what your place is in it. Your beliefs shape your expectations and assumptions, what you think you are capable of; impel you to interact with the world in a particular way or not, and, accordingly, create your experience of life and the world around you.

Your beliefs empower you and support your hopes and dreams, and you can create a whole world of possibilities; or they can be limiting or paralyzing, and hold you back.

Your Values Related to Money

Your values are formed directly from your early beliefs, which are formed by your early life experiences and messages about money.

Your values reflect the people, places, things and concepts that you believe are most important and without which you cannot be your best and most brilliant, passionate Self! Your values are deeply-held personal beliefs about what you regard as important, worthy, desirable or right.

Your values tend to reflect your upbringing, and change very little without conscious effort. Fortunately with increased

Couples and Money: Cracking the code to ending the #1 conflict in marriage

consciousness, awareness and mindfulness, your beliefs and values can change during your life.

In the early years of their marriage, John believed that it was *unnecessary* for Barb to have "a lot of shoes." He believed that a few pairs of shoes should be plenty for all eventualities. John believed that buying shoes for specific outfits or for specific kinds of clothes (for example, casual jeans, dressy jeans, casual dresses and business clothes) was wasteful.

Barb didn't even relate to the word *necessary*. It was unthinkable to wear the same pair of shoes with all her jeans, or with casual dresses she might wear on the weekends, and with business suits and dresses she would wear to work.

For John, the fact that they could easily afford all the shoes that Barb "thought she needed" was completely irrelevant.

When John and Barb started to work with me they were hopelessly deadlocked. In a short time they started to understand how their early life experiences and family messages about money contributed to their current beliefs about money and their different spending behaviors. Now John is able to join Barb in her excitement when she buys new shoes; and Barb is more conscious about her spending behaviors.

That which you value will influence how you think about money, and how you spend and how you save your money.

Let me say that a different way: Your values about money will drive your behavior with money.

4

Realize Conflicts by Recognizing How Your Past Influences
Your Financial Present and Future

What are your values related to money? What do you want money for?

To help you determine your values consider these questions:

1. If you had all the money you needed, what would you do with your life?

2. If you found out you had 10 years to live, what would you do with those 10 years?

3. If you found out you had 24 hours left to live, what would you regret?

Your Attitudes about Money

Your attitudes are aligned with your values and, at the same time, are much more flexible than your values.

You may hold an attitude that you want or need to have more money than you can ever spend; or you may complain about the rising cost of everything, and even become inflamed if you buy something for one price and soon after see it in the same store at a much-reduced price.

Your Behaviors Related to Money

Behaviors or actions with money are aligned with your values and are strongly related to your goals that are driven by your values. What you believe is important will lead you to make certain decisions and to behave in certain ways. Sound money management (responsible behaviors with money) begins with financial goals that are Specific, Measurable, Achievable, Results-Oriented, and Time-Bound (SMART).

Couples and Money: Cracking the code to ending the #1 conflict in marriage

John was an ardent saver and was planning to begin investing in the very near future. Remember John's father used to say, "Money doesn't grow on trees, my boy!" "A penny saved is a penny earned." "Time is money." "Never spend your money before you have it."

Barb didn't have an opinion about saving one way or the other and sometimes she thought John was a bit of a bully with her about saving and investing money.

Again, after an exploration of early beliefs, experiences and family messages, both John and Barb came to recognize and understand their personal beliefs and John's strong needs related to saving and investing money.

When John fully understood why and how he had been influenced earlier in his life, his passion about saving and investing was compelling to Barb and they developed a plan that they could both get excited about and commit to.

Successfully Challenge and Change Your Early Beliefs about Money

You hold inaccurate (early) beliefs about what you are capable of doing now and in the future – and those inaccurate beliefs are seriously limiting you.

The truth is that your beliefs are only descriptions of what you are doing right now and they have no relevance to what you might do in the future or what might be possible in the future!

You can't change your beliefs if you don't know what they are.

6

Realize Conflicts by Recognizing How Your Past Influences
Your Financial Present and Future

Grab a piece of paper and write down as many beliefs as you can think of about money.

Then use this 10-Step Belief Inquiry process to begin challenging and changing each one of your early beliefs, one by one.

Let's start with the first belief on your list. Write it down at the top of a second piece of paper.

Now ask yourself these 10 questions about the first belief:

1. What is the worst thing that could happen IF this belief were true?
2. IF this belief were true, is this belief always true?
3. How do I know?
4. Is it true for everyone?
5. Has there ever been a time when it wasn't true?
6. How has holding this belief served me?
7. What thoughts are associated with this belief?
8. What feelings or emotional reactions do I notice?
9. What body sensations am I aware of?
10. What might happen if I changed just one thing I was doing or not doing?

Now go through this same exercise with every belief about money that is on your list.

This exercise will provide lots of rich information about your beliefs and serve as the starting point for you to decide which beliefs serve you and which ones are getting in your way or limiting your choices and decisions about money.

7

Now that you have a list of your beliefs and rich detail about each one, you can begin to change the ones that don't serve you.

Understand that when you make just one change somewhere in your habituated behavior, that one change can open up the possibility for other changes to be possible. Over time, your beliefs will change to reflect your new experiences.

And shifting your limiting beliefs can be as simple as deciding one day that particular beliefs no longer serve you, and then choosing new beliefs to replace them.

Successfully Challenge and Change Your Values about Money

Let's get honest for a minute. Here is a list of positive and negative values associated with money. Which values related to money most closely describe you?

Charitable	Lazy	Responsible
Miserly	Honest	Irresponsible
Frugal	Dishonest	Satisfied
Wasteful	Independent	Envious
Generous	Controlling	Jealous
Hard-working	Resourceful	Selfish

If you identified one or more negative values most closely associated with you, don't despair! Here's the good news! In the presence of this new knowledge, you can decide to change your value(s) about money, and start behaving (making decisions about money) in ways that are congruent with the new positive value(s).

Realize Conflicts by Recognizing How Your Past Influences
Your Financial Present and Future

Successfully Challenge and Change Your Attitudes about Money

Attitudes are ideas that you hold to be true for you, sometimes consciously and sometimes outside your conscious awareness. Your attitudes may not be true for everyone, or even for everyone in your family.

And even so, you don't want your attitudes questioned or challenged by others, but you can certainly tolerate challenging them yourself!

If you examine some of your attitudes about money and discover through this process that you hold limiting attitudes, just as with beliefs and values, you can challenge them and change them.

For example: You become inflamed if you buy something for one price and soon after see it in the same store at a much-reduced price.

Fact #1: You made the purchase at the time and were willing to pay the price you paid. Or did you consider that?

Fact #2: You determined that the article was worth it. Or did you?

Fact #3: You understood that sales occur before and after holidays and seasons, and that the price of merchandise is often reduced. Or did you?

If you take a little time to sort through the facts, your awareness related to your attitude, and the practical reality of the particular situation, you would very likely be able to easily change your attitude.

9

Successfully Challenge and Change Your Behaviors Related to Money

You can't change your behaviors if you don't know what they are. Grab a piece of paper and write down as many behaviors as you can think of related to money (choices and decisions about money). Clearly articulate a behavior.

For example: I don't like buying myself new clothes very often and, when I do, I don't need much (most likely this was John's mindset).

Ask yourself what you believe to be true about money that is contributing to this behavior.

"Money doesn't grow on trees. It takes hard work to make money."

Then use this 5-Step Process to begin to challenge and change each of your behaviors:

1. How has this belief contributed positively to my behaviors around money this month?
2. What is the evidence that this belief about money is true for me?
3. Whose belief is this? Mine? Someone else's?
4. Why do I believe this belief is true?
5. Do I have any desire to change this belief and, consequently, behave differently?

Now make a list of behaviors or actions you can take that will anchor these new beliefs.

Realize Conflicts by Recognizing How Your Past Influences
Your Financial Present and Future

If you are serious about making changes in your behaviors, you need to practice the new behaviors over and over again.

For example:

- Old Limiting Belief: I am not good at managing my money.

- New Belief: I can manage my money rather well.

- Action: Take a look at my checkbook; get it up to date; make an appointment with a Financial Advisor and get some good information about investing.

Make Sustainable Changes in Everyday Money Decisions

Consider that making decisions is a process, and the more you make decisions, the better you get at making good decisions. Children in most families throughout the world have parents who believe it is up to them to tell children what to do, when to do it and how to do it. While this might be easier for parents in the short-term, it is decidedly NOT facilitative of people engaging in the decision-making process: that is, making decisions, living in the often unintended consequences of those decisions, and, more importantly, eventually learning how to trust themselves and their judgment.

It might help you to understand more about general decision-making strategies before you embark on making any kind of change in your decisions about money.

The first thing to consider is "How are YOU impacted and affected by making this decision?" This question is specifically related to who you are in the deepest part of yourself: not who you wish you

Couples and Money: Cracking the code to ending the #1 conflict in marriage

were, or who others may wish you were. At the end of the day, does this decision match who you know yourself to be?

The second thing to consider is "How is your partner/family impacted and affected by making this decision?" This question is specifically related to your understanding that you are part of a whole, and as an adult part of the whole, it is your job to "do no harm" to those you love!

Decision making is an intentional and deliberate process that requires that you engage your brain and think about long-term and short-term intended and unintended consequences related to your decision.

The first decision I invite you to make is to decide to STOP and ask yourself about spending money <u>before</u> you give someone your credit card, write someone a check or hand someone cash.

Ask yourself:

- *How do I benefit from this decision (to spend this money or obligate myself to this debt), long-term and short-term? Or do I?*
- *How do they benefit from this decision (to spend this money or obligate myself to this debt), long-term and short-term? Or do they?*

Whenever you engage in a healthy decision-making process, you are guaranteed that each decision/choice you make will support you to be your best and most brilliant, passionate Self; and with deliberate intention, you will build the life and the love life you want.

Realize Conflicts by Recognizing How Your Past Influences
Your Financial Present and Future

You will learn to decide to make decisions that are beneficial to you and those around you, in the present, in the immediate future, and in the more distant future.

It is essential to good decision making that you continually assess what's going on.

Ask yourself: "Is what I am doing getting me where I want to go?"

If the answer is not a resounding "YES!" then you probably need to make a different decision.

"Money will buy you a pretty good dog, but it won't buy the wag of his tail."

Henry Wheeler Shaw

Chapter 2

UNDERSTAND YOUR MONEY PSYCHOLOGY AND DIFFERENCES THAT CAUSE CONFLICT

As partners building a life together, you don't realize that the tried and true business principles that successful business people have depended on for decades are the same principles that will support you in talking about money, making decisions about money, and in enabling you to make your dreams come true.

Managing your money with your partner is one of the basic fundamental requirements of being a healthy, committed couple. And guess what? It doesn't make a bit of difference if you have more money than you can ever spend in a lifetime or if you don't have any discretionary income at all.

Here are the good reasons that money issues come up in your marriage:

You and your partner have...

- Different earning capabilities and ideas about money earned;
- Different spending habits;
- Different savings goals;
- Different thoughts and ideas about investing;
- Different fears about being poor, and fantasies about being rich!

Couples and Money: Cracking the code to ending the #1 conflict in marriage

There is one sure thing: Financial problems will eventually surface in your marriage. Couples bicker more about money than about practically anything else. No surprise, then, that when money is tight, the battles can really heat up.

People are preoccupied with money. Making money, losing money, earning money, gambling money, saving money for retirement (or a boat, car, house, vacation)–our ideas and beliefs about money permeate our lives.

Single, married, separated or divorced–whatever your situation, it's essential to do some self-examination to understand your attitudes toward money and how they impact your relationship.

We call this your Money Psychology or Money Scripting!

The Psychology of Money

Prosperity and Poverty Thinking are at the core of your Money Psychology.

Your Money Psychology includes how your beliefs, expectations and feelings influence your financial behavior, success, or disappointment.

This means that financial success is an "inside job" and is more determined by what's between your ears and inside your heart than by what's outside of you.

Understand Your Money Psychology and Differences That Cause Conflict

Money Scripts

Money Scripts are beliefs about money that reside in your unconscious mind. They guide your every decision, and they inform your every behavior related to money, and to buying goods and services.

Your beliefs are based on assumptions that you started forming very early in your childhood. Money Scripts can range from "Money is the root of all evil," "Money doesn't grow on trees," "It takes a penny to earn a penny," "It takes hard work to make money," "You can marry rich as easily as you can marry poor;" and on and on.

Prosperity Thinking or Abundance Scripting

If you have a basic, fundamental attitude that at the end of the day you k-n-o-w that "things will work out" you are operating from an internal base known as Prosperity Thinking. When your beliefs, expectations, feelings and attitudes about money are aligned with realistic levels of abundance, optimism, and self-confidence, again, you are operating from an internal base known as Prosperity Thinking or Abundance Scripting.

This alignment generates empowering behavior and a self-fulfilling prophecy that leads to success. More than about how much money you have, Prosperity Thinking or Abundance Scripting is related to you taking charge of your ability to attract money and to create success—energetically and enthusiastically.

Couples and Money: Cracking the code to ending the #1 conflict in marriage

Poverty Thinking or Scarcity Scripting

If you have a basic, fundamental attitude that people and events outside you can't be trusted, or your thinking process is rooted in fear vs. all things are possible all the time, you are operating from an internal base known as Poverty Thinking or Scarcity Scripting. This way of seeing the world, and yourself in it, severely limits you and shuts down many, if not all, possibilities and opportunities you no doubt have: it frequently results in your believing that things will not work out.

Poverty Thinking causes you to be anxious and uncomfortable about money in general, and even the mere notion of financial independence or an absence of struggle, is incomprehensible.

Scarcity Scripting is not related to not having any money! Would you be shocked to know that lots of rich people worry constantly about losing money or not having enough money?

Poverty Thinking or Scarcity Scripting is disempowering because it aligns your beliefs, expectations and feelings with unrealistic levels of scarcity, pessimism, and fear.

Money is a big area in which your early childhood experiences and family messages have created strong emotions and often completely irrational behavior. That's why, no matter how much money you earn or save, or how many solid investments you have, if you are operating from a base of Poverty Thinking or Scarcity Scripting, you will very likely have serious challenges with money.

18

Money is Neutral

It's important to realize that money itself is not the culprit. Money is neutral; it's just pieces of paper, plastic, or electronic digits. The real source of your money issues is what money represents: the meanings you have made about money; having it or not having it; what is enough, and so forth.

Exploring your Money Psychology or your Money Scripting helps you to become more aware of your money issues, how you might sabotage yourself, how you can create more success around money and will help facilitate your ability to have authentic conversations with your partner around money.

Money is a microcosm of your life and your marriage. Although Psychology of Money emphasizes money, please understand that the same mind set and energy that creates financial success or not is also directly related to the quality of your personal and business relationships, your parenting, your physical and emotional well-being, your decisions about how to create and enjoy leisure time, your creativity, intuition, intimacy,…it shows up everywhere in your life!

Let's shift gears for a moment and examine how and why you may spend money, or not.

According to social learning theory, spending behaviors can be viewed as learned behavior that is passed from generation to generation.

According to psychologists D'Astous and Forties, "spending behaviors and their patterns have been conceived as existing along a continuum running between two poles. One pole represents the "holding on" behaviors or a preoccupation with the acquisition and hoarding of money while the other pole represents the obsessive spending of money."

In the financial planning world and the relationship coaching world, spending behaviors commonly fall into recognizable categories from Hoarders to Obsessive Spenders.

Hoarders

Men and women who can't part with their money–who fiercely fight against spending money on themselves or others for any reason–are known as Hoarders.

Yvonne Kaye, the author of *Credit, Cash and Codependency* writes: "Hoarders live by the phrase, 'But, I might need it someday.' Many hoarders lived through the Depression, the Holocaust, or some other conflict where there was really no money to buy goods and services, and even IF you had a little money, there were barely any goods or services to buy. These people were truly not able to meet their families' needs."

Under-Spenders

Under-spenders represent the most extreme condition of hoarding. These men and women resist spending, even when it will result in dire consequences for themselves or others in their lives. These folks will refuse to go to a doctor or a hospital if they or someone they dearly love is seriously ill. They refuse to buy seasonal clothes to accommodate the change in temperature.

Understand Your Money Psychology and Differences That Cause Conflict

Spenders or Amassers

Now we are moving to the other side of the spectrum–to Spenders or Amassers.

This spending behavior is reserved for those who have created enormous wealth and who spend money for the pure joy of spending, and for the love of owning beautiful clothes, art, jewels, traveling, and the like.

You've probably heard the old phrase "Spendthrift" or heard someone say of another: "She spends money like water" or "She buys like it is going out of style."

These references were no doubt referring to Spenders and Amassers.

Over-Spenders

Now we have arrived at a very serious spending behavior–Overspending.

The people who overspend do so because possessions give them identity. They believe that they will be happy and life will be everything they ever hoped and dreamed it would be IF they just had that designer purse; or took that luxury cruise; or bought that exotic car. And of course, nothing could be farther from the truth.

Overspending can be writing checks to buy something you believe you must have when the money in the checking account is to pay the rent or to buy food; the indiscriminate use of credit cards because you "want it," even though you have no way of paying for it l-a-t-e-r; or the need to spend money to create a mood change.

21

Kaye says: "Buying is their only way to feel good. It is their fix."

Spending works as a kind of anesthetic for the deep pain that lives inside people who don't like themselves very much and who always compare themselves to others and come up short; people who lack a connection to their personal gifts, skills and talents; and who live their lives without a plan or a direction.

Over-spenders live in a debtor's prison of their own making. The very shame that torments them and comes from their out-of-control spending is the same energy that compels them to do it over and over again.

For people with extreme hoarding or spending patterns, it is important to stress that recovery from these behaviors is very much like recovery from other substance abuse. Don't think for a minute this is about "how to handle your money." This recovery process must be integrated with work to improve one's sense of self-worth and self-esteem.

When money is tight, expect people to become anxious and know they will revert strongly to type: hoarders will save more passionately; spenders will spend more passionately.

Within the context of a marriage, what can couples do to be able to talk about money in a way that makes sense; that will be helpful and will actually reduce conflict between them?

Understand Your Money Psychology and Differences That Cause Conflict

Here is a short process to begin sorting where the problem might be:

1. Understand your spending behaviors.

2. Understand your partner's spending behaviors.

3. Identify where your behaviors fall on the continuum between the two extremes of hoarding and spending.

4. Identify where you think your partner's behaviors fall on the continuum between the two extremes of hoarding and spending.

5. Evaluate how much of a problem you think your own hoarding or spending is contributing to the money issues that come up in your marriage.

6. Evaluate how much of a problem you think your partner's hoarding or spending is contributing to the money issues that come up in your marriage.

This short exercise will give you and your partner lots of good information and a solid place on which to begin to build. Next, examine as honestly as you can, what family rules and family messages deeply informed your beliefs and attitudes about money, and recognize how those beliefs and attitudes are very likely operating everyday outside your conscious awareness.

"Before you speak, listen. Before you write, think. Before you spend, earn. Before you invest, investigate. Before you criticize, wait. Before you pray, forgive. Before you quit, try. Before you retire, save. Before you die, give."

William A. Ward

Chapter 3

AVOID CONFLICT BY UNDERSTANDING THE ENERGY OF MONEY

Whatever you believe is true…is!

If you believe that money is the root of all evil, then your belief will be reflected back to you in many ways and will deepen your belief that you are right.

If you believe that the Universe pays for passion and it is your personal obligation to follow your passion, then your belief will be reflected back to you in many ways, and will deepen your belief that you are right.

Many of your beliefs and convictions about money are widely assumed to be true, and are in fact, patently wrong; yet most people accept them without question!

You learned these beliefs and assumptions from your parents, teachers, books, television and the media; you hold these beliefs and assumptions consciously and unconsciously, and they now directly impact and affect how you think about and relate to money.

The whole area of money has a powerful emotional charge! Almost everyone wants more money or enough money, yet the very idea of having a lot of money often carries with it terribly negative connotations–negative energy.

25

On one hand, money is highly desirable and highly valued: on the other hand, money is considered bad and sometimes evil.

You Give Money Its Energy!

Here's the truth about money: U.S. currency paper used to be composed of 25 percent linen and 75 percent cotton, with red and blue synthetic fibers of various lengths distributed evenly throughout it. Before World War I these fibers were made of silk.

Today, the paper used to print bills is a special kind of grass. U.S. coins are pure copper in the middle with an outer layer of copper and nickel combined.

Money has no natural energy. You give money its energy. And when money issues are emotionally charged, the charge is directly related to you–not to the money itself!

Consider that money is a medium of exchange: the exchange is all about energy and money, as a concept, symbolizes the exchange of energy.

Money is energy made visible.

Money is neither good nor bad, nor moral or immoral. It is an inanimate object just like a car or an airplane. To take another view is as illogical as it is to decide that cars are good or bad.

We feel differently about cars when they are used to drive children to school than when they are used as get-away vehicles from a bank robbery. Yet they are the same cars. The focus is the intention of the user–not in the car itself.

26

Money can be used to deepen and to enrich the opportunities of life, or it can be used to harm others or spoil events.

Explore Common Clichés and Build New Beliefs about Money

Have you ever noticed all the clichés and notions that send the message that there is something wrong with money itself, with wanting money, and something really wrong with you if you have it. Or what about the message that if you had money everything would be okay? Here is a list of a few you might be familiar with. At the end of this list, take a moment to add any clichés or old limiting beliefs that live inside your head that I have not listed:

- *Money is the root of all evil (the actual quote is "The love of money is the root of all evil").*
- *Money won't buy you happiness.*
- *Easy come, easy go.*
- *If I could only win the lottery all my problems would be solved.*
- *Filthy rich.*
- *He sold his soul...*
- *I may be poor, but I'm happy.*
- *Money doesn't grow on trees!*
- *I can't afford that!*
- *You can't be rich and spiritual!*
- *If only I had more money, I'd be happy.*
- *Rich people are greedy and dishonest!*
- *If I'm wealthy, my friends will be jealous and stop liking me!*

Couples and Money: Cracking the code to ending the #1 conflict in marriage

- *I'm not smart enough to be rich!*
- *If I'm financially successful, I won't know how to handle the money.*
- *You have to be born with money to be wealthy.*
- *It takes money to make money.*
- *Money goes to money.*
- *When I'm rich, I won't have to put up with this...*
- *It's just as easy to marry rich as marry poor.*
- *People won't like me if I'm wealthy.*
- *You have to spend money to make money.*
- *Money can't buy you love.*
- *My friends and family will reject me if I'm wealthy.*
- *If I'm rich, someone else will have to be poor.*
- *Money talks.*
- *Spiritual people don't care about money.*
- *In order to be wealthy you have to work all the time and sacrifice your health, your family, and your leisure activities.*
- *Financial success isn't worth the price.*
- *In order to be wealthy you have to lie, cheat, and steal.*
- *Wealthy people are selfish and shallow and don't care about others.*
- *I can't get what I want.*
- *You have to marry a rich man to be a rich woman.*

This list of limiting beliefs can go on and on. Understand that limiting beliefs block the flow of (financial) abundance from flowing into your life. Your money beliefs are your blueprint

28

for financial success or failure. Your money beliefs are directly related to your level of financial abundance and your willingness or ability to receive that abundance!

Because you are reading this book, you are light-years ahead of most people who never do any critical thinking or exploring about what they believe, why they believe what they do, and how they are being positively or negatively impacted and affected by their beliefs.

Change False Beliefs and Assumptions about Money

Your false beliefs and assumptions, and all the myths about money that you allow in and operate from, as if they were the truth, are not just personal beliefs: they are strong threads in the fabric of every culture throughout the world today.

You did not get here all by yourself.
But you must get out of here all alone!

You must root them out, and stop believing them so you can start living from the truth and free yourself from their limiting and negative influence.

If you have limiting beliefs that are conscious and unconscious, you can transform them into productive, positive and powerful beliefs to create wealth and abundance every day of your life.

Fortunately, you are the creator of your beliefs, values, attitudes and "self-talk." It is up to you to decide to remind yourself every day to embrace positive, empowering beliefs and attitudes about money and its value to you.

29

Couples and Money: Cracking the code to ending the #1 conflict in marriage

Observe what you have in your life and know with clarity and certainty that if whatever you believe, think and assume on the inside, even if you don't know you believe, think or assume these things, is massively affecting you and your life! You create your outside existential life in your own image whether or not your images are hopelessly distorted or exquisitely accurate.

Contemporary societies all over the world have it wrong! And when you follow their example, you have it all wrong too. Take a look at some common expressions that you hear all the time—expressions or variations that are probably running through and deeply informing your thought process and decision-making process related to money every day:

- *It's a dog-eat-dog world.*
- *You have to fight to survive.*
- *It's either him or me.*
- *A small group of people control all the money.*
- *The squeaky wheel gets the grease.*
- *It's a jungle out there.*
- *Heads I win, tails you lose.*
- *The world is not a friendly place.*
- *Welcome to the real world.*

The very idea that you must live on a power continuum, that there is not enough, and that you have to fight for what's yours, is an example of the most rampant kind of Scarcity Thinking! It is an indelible imprint on your mind that there is a limit on the amount of money that you can earn or have.

30

Avoid Conflict By Understanding The Energy Of Money

Scarcity Thinking is a set-up everywhere you look, and leads you to conclude that you have to fight someone for something, and you must compete and win, to get what you want. The Universe is not finite. It isn't necessary to take from someone who has a lot so you can have more. It is inaccurate to believe that one person is of necessity getting less because another is getting more.

That is complete and utter nonsense! Listen up!

You have been told in many ways, over and over, that the world is a finite place and that you can have either principles or money, but not both. We've already dispelled the myth that the Universe is finite. This incomprehensible idea that ideals and money are in opposition to each other is not only completely wrong: it has poisoned your beliefs about what is possible for you! From *Robin Hood* to *The Emperor's New Clothes* and Dickens' *A Christmas Carol*, this myth has been perpetrated on the culture for decades.

The plain fact is that you are the source of your happiness and your unhappiness, regardless of how much money you have!

You are in charge of busting the false myths you hold as truth, and challenging your old, limiting beliefs and assumptions.

Follow this easy exercise to begin this process:

Grab a sheet of paper and draw a vertical line, from top to bottom, down the center of the piece of paper to create two columns. In the left column, write something that you really want. In the right column, write the reason why you don't have it.

31

For example, let's say you really want an iPhone.

In the left column, write iPhone. In the right column, write all the reasons you don't have it (your limiting beliefs).

For example, you may write:

- I can't afford that phone.
- That phone is too expensive for me.
- I don't need a phone like that.
- An iPhone is for a person who has lots of money.
- People will think I am throwing away my money if I bought that phone.
- My friends will think I am trying to be better than them.

Once you identify your limiting beliefs, you can transform them into more accurate powerful beliefs that will support you to really be in charge of creating wealth and abundance. Transforming beliefs can be as simple as deciding that a particular belief no longer serves you, and then choosing a new belief to replace it.

For example:

Perhaps you believe that rich people are selfish and self-centered. If you've worked all your life to be a kind, caring person, you would probably make pretty darn sure that you wouldn't earn lots of money. But when you actually examine your limiting belief and recognize that your belief really isn't accurate, and you conclude that being selfish and self-centered doesn't have anything to do with the amount of money and wealth you have, you could choose to embrace a different belief–perhaps a belief that rich people use their money on behalf of lots of people and do good with their money.

Avoid Conflict By Understanding The Energy Of Money

Abundance and Prosperity Are an Inside Job!

Your thoughts and beliefs affect your willingness and ability to create wealth and abundance!

- Have you closed the doors to prosperity by buying into your old, limiting beliefs and assumptions about money?

- Do you believe that you deserve to be abundant and prosperous?

- Do you daydream about being wealthy and having e-n-o-u-g-h money and at the very same time worry about how you'll pay your bills?

- Money is a resource with a neutral energy onto which you project your beliefs. When you change your limiting beliefs and bust the false myths about money, money changes for you.

Your attitudes about money often match other attitudes you have about the world and your life:

- What is your attitude about giving?

- Do you give freely of yourself?

- When is it easy to give?

- When is it challenging to give?

- Is it hard for you to receive?

Giving and receiving are equal opposites of the same coin.

Are you someone who can give money and give of yourself joyfully, but when someone tries to give you money or give of themselves to you, you push them way?

Couples and Money: Cracking the code to ending the #1 conflict in marriage

Are you someone who can receive money and receive the help, support, and the kindness of others easily and effortlessly, but it is nearly impossible for you to give generously to others, even to charity?

Money is meant to be circulated. That is, money is meant to be given graciously and joyfully and it is meant to be received gratefully and easily. Money is meant to be shared with others.

Stretch your money muscles and get ready to give with joy and enthusiasm and equally ready to receive with gratitude and ease. As you invite and allow money to flow in and out of your life more often, more money will flow in and out of your life.

In a short time you will start attracting the people and events that support your new money beliefs and attitudes, and you'll increase the abundance and prosperity in your life exponentially.

Intentional Decisions and Choices Related to Money

Money cannot make you happy, but intentional decisions and choices related to money can provide the means of unlimited good for you and many others in your life.

- How do you use money?
- What plans or direction do you have in place for your money?
- What seeds are being planted with your money?

Increasing abundance and prosperity can be likened to being a farmer at planting time.

34

Avoid Conflict By Understanding The Energy Of Money

If you have no plans for your land and you simply throw your seeds around indiscriminately, you are wasting your resources, and if you're very lucky, you may wind up with a small crop in return: a crop which will be very challenging to tend if it is scattered all over the place.

Conversely, if you make careful plans about where and when you will plant what, you will have a far better chance to grow a hearty, healthy crop of everything you plant.

Very few people ever consciously and intentionally sit down and think concretely about money or ever ask these questions:

- Are you willing to create the money required to make your dreams come true?
- Are you more or less uncomfortable around money?
- What does "being poor" mean to you?
- What associations/beliefs do you have about wealthy people?
- What associations/beliefs do you have about earning "a lot" of money?
- Do you want to help others with your money?
- At the end of your life, what do you want to have achieved with your money?

If you want to create wealth and prosperity it is essential to pay attention to your internal experience when you earn, spend, give, receive, save and invest money.

Additionally, understand how the laws of prosperity operate in giving, receiving, spending, and saving so you can be proactive on

35

Couples and Money: Cracking the code to ending the #1 conflict in marriage

your own behalf, and effectively direct the movement of money energy.

Abundance and Prosperity require planning; acting with deliberate intention and commitment, and managing your debt.

Money freedom requires that your thoughts, feelings, actions and beliefs about money match—that is, when what you do, think, and say all match each other.

- You'll never be free if you say that you have more than enough money and then behave as if you don't and think you don't.
- You'll never be free if you think you don't have enough money and then act as if you do and say you do.

You will have more than enough money when you believe you will; when you take the appropriate actions that positively express your belief; and when you realize that you can be wealthy no matter how much money you earn, save, spend or invest because you are more than your money, and more than your money can buy.

"Happiness is not in the mere possession of money; it lies in the joy of achievement, in the thrill of creative effort."

Franklin D. Reosevelt

Chapter 4

ALL ABOUT DEBT—ESCAPE
THE CONFLICT

A comprehensive conversation about money in marriage wouldn't be complete without a brief review of the basic elements related to debt and the behaviors of incurring debt.

Every day, couples struggle with the harsh realities and implications of debt. In fact, debt and financial problems cause about 90 percent of divorces in America.

Most couples today are asking themselves whether their relationship can survive pre-marital debt, student loans, mortgage debt, car leases, credit card debt, military debt, and baby boomer debt.

Is Debt Weakening Your Financial Fitness?

- Have you ever spent more money than you made?
- Are you currently spending more money than you make?
- Have you ever spent money you didn't have?
- Are you currently spending money you don't have?

These might sound like ridiculous questions, but if you're spending more money than you make or spending money you don't have, you are weakening your financial fitness. If you are using credit cards, borrowing money from others or dipping into your savings to make ends meet or buying something you really, really want, you are also weakening your financial fitness.

37

Debt isn't something that just happens to you. Your spending habits lead you directly into debt.

You might be able to get away with handling money this way for a short time, but long term these spending behaviors will catch up with you. Before you know it, you don't have money for a rainy day, your savings are depleted or worse; and your credit cards are maxed out.

Recognize your dangerous spending now, and make the changes that will improve and strengthen your financial fitness.

Tell the Truth About Your Money—Intentionally and Regularly!

Partners come into relationships with pre-established spending habits and financial histories; and for many reasons resist talking to each other about money, sometimes for years! So it is no wonder that so many couples wind up in perilous financial circumstances.

Establish and maintain a regular conversation about money, and decide, together, what your spending behaviors and limits will be. Begin by talking about how much money you earn, how much money you need to meet your current expenses, and how much debt you have (from spending more money than you made in the past and/or in the present).

All About Debt--Escape the Conflict

Keeping Spending in Check

Michael and Laura have been married for seven years. They met in college and both had student loans and used credit cards to make ends meet. After college they both got good jobs and paid off their student loans, but the credit card debt continued to mount up. Michael has been very upset with Laura for some time now, and believes she spends too much money on superfluous things and pays too much for what they do need. He nags her incessantly; no matter how much she changes her spending habits, decreases their debt on an on-going basis and keeps her spending in check. One Saturday, not long ago, Michael came home with a BIG surprise: a 70-inch flat-screen plasma TV. He was so excited and very proudly explained how he took advantage of this 'couldn't pass up' deal.

According to a SmartMoney survey, spending is the second most common reason why couples fight. The research and anecdotal stories continue to show that men and women spend the same amount of money: they just spend differently.

Over the years, the old model of money management has generally included the view that, more often than not, women buy groceries, clothes for the children, and take care of expenses related to the household and the family's daily needs.

According to the old model, men have generally been identified as those who make decisions and spend money on large purchases like plasma TVs, cars or computers.

The fact of the matter is that if you kept a spreadsheet over time, it would be clear that men and women spend about the same amount of money–in real dollars and cents. The only thing that

39

is different is the perception, because they spend differently–not more or less.

In a financially fit marriage, spending is mutually agreed to, deliberate and intentional, not unlike so many other agreements between partners.

Credit Cards

One of the fastest ways to get into debt is to choose to use credit cards, either because you don't have enough money to buy what you want to buy, or because you like the idea of *buy now, pay later,* for some reason.

If you don't have the money to buy what you want, you would be well served to curtail your spending. If you use credit instead of cash, recognize that it is a bad habit that could have very serious consequences some day.

Using Debt to Pay Off Debt and Spiraling Debt

When you use credit cards to pay off other cards, and loans to pay off other loans, you're not paying off anything. You're just moving money around and getting deeper into debt.

Balance transfers have transaction fees, and most loans have some kind of down payment or origination fee. Don't think for a moment that when you use debt to pay off debt, you are actually paying off anything. You are really getting in deeper and making an already bad situation worse!

All About Debt--Escape the Conflict

And, if you use a credit card to buy things and miss a payment, then miss another one, or pay off only a small amount, the debt increases every month and spirals out of control.

Taking Out Loans

There is an old saying: "Borrow to invest in an asset. Save to pay expenses."

Assets are good. Once you've paid for them, you have something of value that you could sell if you had to.

Assets or Value Builders are likely to hold their value, grow in value or give you income after you've paid for them. Your home is generally thought to be a value builder.

Buying a value-building asset is an investment and is generally considered to be a valid reason to go into debt.

Unfortunately, too many people borrow money to pay expenses– things that leave you with nothing after you've paid for them. Living costs, nights out, and vacations are all examples of expenses.

Taking loans from friends and family, and making loans to friends and family, can often result in a problem worse than not having the money you need. If you are going to be on either end of this dicey transaction, be sure you make specific agreements that you absolutely intend to honor if you are the borrower; set clear expectations related to when the loan is to be repaid; establish whether there is interest to be paid; and understand what the consequences would be if the loan were not repaid in full on time, and so forth.

41

Here's a Tip from your friendly Relationship Educator: If you are in a position to make the loan, consider making it a gift. If you are borrowing the money, step up and suggest that you sign a legal document. Promissory Notes are available in office supply stores and online.

Emergency Fund

Medical emergencies or the hot water heater bursting on a Sunday morning are not spending decisions that are within your control, and they may negatively affect the best-laid financial plans for a long time!

Professionals in the world of personal finances are always telling us to have a "rainy day fund" or a savings account for emergencies.

When you begin to shift your consciousness from *debt-consciousness* to *wealth-building consciousness*, make this a top priority! It makes sense.

Gambling

For some people, gambling can be as recreational as going to the movies or out for a great meal.

People who gamble recreationally gamble in casinos occasionally, bet on sports, horse races, car races, and online occasionally; and millions of people buy lottery tickets.

Recreational and problem gambling are NOT the same.

All About Debt--Escape the Conflict

Debate exists over how problem gambling is defined, but generally, it is defined as any gambling that causes harm, in any way, to the gambler or to someone else. Problem gambling is gambling behavior that causes disruptions in any major area of life: psychological, physical, social or vocational.

It is a progressive addiction characterized by increasing preoccupation with gambling, a need to bet more money more frequently, restlessness or irritability when attempting to stop, "chasing" losses, and loss of control manifested by continuation of the gambling behavior in spite of mounting, serious, negative consequences.

Gamblers Anonymous offers the following questions to anyone who may have a gambling problem. These questions are provided to help the individual decide whether or not he or she is a compulsive gambler who wants to stop gambling.

1. Did you ever lose time from work or school due to gambling?
2. Has gambling ever made your home life unhappy?
3. Has gambling affected your reputation?
4. Have you ever felt remorse after gambling?
5. Have you ever gambled to get money with which to pay debts or otherwise solve financial difficulties?
6. Has gambling caused a decrease in your ambition or efficiency?
7. After losing, have you felt that you had to return as soon as possible and win back your losses?
8. After a win, did you have a strong urge to return and win more?

Couples and Money: Cracking the code to ending the #1 conflict in marriage

9. Do you often gamble until your last dollar was gone?

10. Do you ever borrow to finance your gambling?

11. Have you ever sold anything to finance gambling?

12. Have you been reluctant to use "gambling money" for normal expenditures?

13. Has gambling made you careless of the welfare of yourself or your family?

14. Have you ever gambled longer than you had planned?

15. Have you ever gambled to escape worry, trouble, boredom or loneliness?

16. Have you ever committed, or considered committing, an illegal act to finance gambling?

17. Has gambling caused you to have difficulty in sleeping?

18. Do arguments, disappointments or frustrations create within you an urge to gamble?

19. Have you ever had an urge to celebrate any good fortune by a few hours of gambling?

20. Have you ever considered self-destruction or suicide as a result of your gambling?

Most compulsive gamblers will answer "yes" to at least seven of these questions.

According to the APA (American Psychiatric Association) pathological gambling is an impulse disorder that is a chronic and progressive mental illness and, interestingly enough, the 10 symptoms included in this diagnosis closely mirror the questions posed by Gamblers Anonymous.

Values, Attitudes, Beliefs and Habits Related to Managing Money

"Your financial life is like a garden. If you tend a garden carefully, nourishing the flowers, pruning, and weeding, it's going to be a lot more beautiful than if you just water it halfheartedly now and then."

Suze Orman

Chapter 5

VALUES, ATTITUDES, BELIEFS AND HABITS RELATED TO MANAGING MONEY, BUILDING WEALTH AND PREVENTING CONFLICT

Before you can explore and actually make any changes to the way you manage money, you must have a comprehensive understanding about where you are now. What values, attitudes, beliefs and habits (behaviors) do you hold, and act on, now?

Your Values

What do you want out of life? What matters to you...really matters to you?

I want to suggest that you set a course to improve your financial fitness by making financial decisions that are in alignment with your core values.

The real truth is that you live according to a set of values; and you continually behave in a way that reflects your values. Values drive behavior!

Values are ideas–about the worth of people, concepts, or objects– that come from beliefs.

Sometimes your values are related more to the values of others you love and respect. Part of your work is to sort out your values, to own the ones that are yours, and to create a

47

Couples and Money: Cracking the code to ending the #1 conflict in marriage

personal life, a love life and a financial life that match your core values!

So, if you value paying your financial obligations on time, you will honor this value by behaving in ways that ensure the timeliness of your payment.

Knowing what you value and honoring your values; behaving in accordance with those values, energizes everything and everybody involved.

You have a set of between four and six primary values that are the underpinnings of your life. There may be other values that you hold and honor in the course of your life and which are demonstrated through your behavior and your choices, but they are secondary to your primary core values.

Would you be surprised to learn that your financial problems are the product of you not recognizing your values, you not paying careful attention to these values, and/or you being completely unaware that you even hold such values?

Advertisers depend on you not being aware of your values. Through advertising methods, advertisers express a core value that some people have; represent it as a core value that all people have, and make their product seem essential to honoring that value!

Below is a list of some of the most common values. You'll recognize some of these as important to YOU, and most of the others will be less important.

48

Values, Attitudes, Beliefs and Habits Related to Managing Money,
Building Wealth and Preventing Conflict

Needs and Values

Accomplishment	Achievement	Accountability
Accuracy	Adventure	All for one and one for all
Beauty	Calm, Quietude	Challenge
Change	Cleanliness	Commitment
Communication	Community	Competition
Concern for others	Content over form	Continuous improvement
Cooperation	Coordination	Country
Creativity	Decisiveness	Discipline
Discovery	Efficiency	Excellence
Fairness	Faith	Family
Freedom	Friendship	Fun
Gratitude	Hard work	Harmony
Honesty	Honor	Inner peace
Innovation	Compassion	Inspiration
Competence	Integrity	Justice
Knowledge	Looking after yourself	Love, Romance
Loyalty	Meaning	Merit
Money	Openness	Orderliness
Passion	Peace, Non-violence	Positive attitude
Personal Growth	Pleasure	Practicality
Preservation	Privacy	Prosperity
Punctuality	Quiet	Resourcefulness
Respect for individual	Safety	Satisfying others
Security	Self-care	Self-reliance
Self-respect	Self-worth	Service (to others or society)
Simplicity	Spirit in life (using)	Stability
Strength	Success	Tradition
Tranquility	Trust	Truth
Unity	Wealth	Wisdom

Your Beliefs and Attitudes

A belief is any cognitive content that a person holds as true regarding people, concepts, or objects, including himself or herself.

What you see, hear, read, reflect upon and experience causes you to develop an opinion (belief) about something–money, in this case. This belief gives you an understanding or misunderstanding, which in turn, allows you to decide what its (money's) worth is to you (the value).

49

Couples and Money: Cracking the code to ending the #1 conflict in marriage

The value you place on money, or something you want to buy with your money, is not always in alignment with your core values if your core values are not clearly recognized and being honored by you.

You can successfully challenge and change deeply held beliefs, if you understand the origins of your beliefs and recognize that they can be changed.

Know that you can achieve all that you set out to do for yourself. You only need to start believing in yourself.

An attitude is generally defined as a way of looking at life; a way of thinking, feeling and behaving. An attitude is your feeling or mood toward people, events and circumstances.

Your attitude is a complex mental state that is driven by your values and beliefs; and involves your perceptions of yourself and people, events and circumstances in your life.

Your attitude = your feelings + your thoughts + your actions.

So, your attitude isn't just the way you think, but includes the way you think, feel and behave.

Attitude, whether positive or negative, shows in your daily life. Many people say attitude is more important than experience or education. Attitude is often considered as the tiebreaker between two equally qualified candidates.

Let's examine the difference between a belief about money and an attitude to money by looking more closely at Martin's behavior.

Martin holds a **belief** that smart money management is essential to attain financial security for his family and for his retirement.

Martin demonstrates his **attitude** toward the importance of saving when he speaks to younger members of the team about the importance of saving money; when he brings lunch to work or routinely chooses less expensive restaurants at which to eat during the lunch hour; and when he ensures that a certain percentage of his money goes directly into a special savings plan each month.

You choose your attitude. You alone can decide how to view, perceive and relate to people, events and circumstances in your life.

Your Habits

A habit is a pattern of behavior that occurs automatically. Habits are routines of behavior that are repeated regularly, and occur subconsciously without directly thinking, or deciding or being intentional about them.

Habitual or habituated behavior goes unnoticed because you are engaging in behavior routinely, outside your conscious awareness, so you aren't going to become self-examining or reflective or introspective. You will simply behave exactly as you always have and complete routine tasks without noticing or challenging yourself. You do the same things you did yesterday, the day before and every day for the last month and the last year, and so on.

It is estimated that our brains only consciously process 40 out of every 11,000 signals we receive from our senses.

Couples and Money: Cracking the code to ending the #1 conflict in marriage

So here's the good news! Habits, good or bad, make you who you are. The key is controlling them; and changing habits–even the most formidable spending habits–is completely doable! If you know how to change your habits, then even a small effort can create a big change.

Earning Your Money

What is your value for working and earning money?

Is it important to you to take the time to learn what your natural gifts and talents are and then to find ways to share them with the world through your work? And if so, do you support your partner in doing the same thing?

Do you believe that it is important to get in touch with what is really important to you; and to create a fulfilling career; to do something you love that fits who you are so you can be your best and most brilliant, passionate Self?

Or do you believe that you work to make money and seeking to enjoy your work is frivolous?

Do you subscribe to the school of thought that suggests that when you are happy in your work life that satisfaction and happiness positively affects other parts of your life?

Do you agree that it is a better choice to be esteemed and affirmed by the work you do and to live more joyfully and healthfully in the present than it is to be waiting for the day you get to retire so that you can begin to be happy?

Values, Attitudes, Beliefs and Habits Related to Managing Money,
Building Wealth and Preventing Conflict

Being aware of what you think and believe about earning money will be helpful in later chapters when we focus on you and your partner *Building the Family Business*.

Spending Your Money

In Chapter 2 we explored spending habits: hoarders, under-spenders, amassers and over-spenders.

Do you recall which spending habit you related to most closely?

I think it is important to stress again that when money is tight, expect yourself to become anxious and know you will revert strongly to type: hoarders will save more passionately; spenders will spend more passionately.

Make it a point to sit down with your partner and discuss what is going on with your money, and make spending decisions together to strengthen your financial fitness.

Let's review this process:

1. Understand your spending behaviors.
2. Understand your partner's spending behaviors.
3. Identify where your behaviors fall on the continuum between the two extremes of hoarding and spending.
4. Identify where you think your partner's behaviors fall on the continuum between the two extremes of hoarding and spending.
5. Evaluate how much of a problem you think your own hoarding or spending is contributing to the money issues that come up in your marriage.

53

Couples and Money: Cracking the code to ending the #1 conflict in marriage

6. Evaluate how much of a problem you think your partner's hoarding or spending is contributing to the money issues that come up in your marriage.

Remember, you can change any spending behavior, no matter how formidable it is, with conscious effort and a specific plan.

Understanding as much as possible about your spending behaviors will be helpful in later chapters when we focus on you and your partner **Building the Family Business**.

Accounting for Your Money

What's your personal experience with accounting for (or managing) your money? Is it part of your personal financial fitness plan? Is it something you avoid; or perhaps you don't think about managing your money at all?

How did your parents and grandparents manage money?

Accounting for money requires that you stop putting your head in the sand and stop avoiding knowing exactly the state of your finances.

Accounting for your money (or money management) is the process of knowing where you are spending your money today, and having a well thought-out plan in place for how you want to spend your money in the future.

This requires deliberate intention and attention to how much you are earning, what your expenses are, how much debt you have, and how much you are going to save and invest.

Values, Attitudes, Beliefs and Habits Related to Managing Money,
Building Wealth and Preventing Conflict

Budgeting is an approach to keeping track of all these details. Budgeting involves understanding how much money you earn and spend over a period of time. When you create a budget, you are creating a plan for spending and saving money.

Think of your budget as a "spending plan," a way to be aware of how much money you have, where it needs to go, and how much is left over and what you want to do with it.

Most people equate budgeting with deprivation. Nothing could be further from the truth. A budget supports the financial fitness plan you develop, and meets your "needs" first, then the "wants" that you can afford.

Theoretically, your expenses are less than or equal to your total income. If your income is not enough to cover your expenses, adjust your budget (and your spending!) by deciding which expenses can be reduced.

Accounting for your money, or managing your money, is an essential part of creating your best life for the rest of your life.

Recognizing your attitude about money management and being honest about your experience–that is, actually accounting for your money–will be helpful in later chapters when we focus on you and your partner ***Building the Family Business***.

55

Couples and Money: Cracking the code to ending the #1 conflict in marriage

Saving Your Money

What was your family's value about saving money?

How old were you when you opened your first savings account? Whatever happened to that money?

Pay yourself first! Have you ever heard that old adage?

Saving is really a very important part of protecting you financially, and yet only a very small percentage of people save money on a regular basis.

A good rule of thumb is to save as much as you can every month. Saving even a very small amount of money can make a big difference if you keep it up.

The vast majority of people save money if there is anything left at the end of the month to save.

That really isn't how it works!

Saving begins as a mind-set that is supported by intentional behavior.

Pay yourself first. When you pay your monthly bills, write out a check to you, and deposit it into your savings account FIRST, or ask your employer to directly deposit some of your paycheck into your savings account.

If you don't hold a strong belief about saving that drives a behavior to save, then experiment with saving a few dollars a week at first.

56

Values, Attitudes, Beliefs and Habits Related to Managing Money,
Building Wealth and Preventing Conflict

While walking to a Starbucks for coffee decide not to go, and, instead, take the $3.40 (cash) and deposit it in your savings account. That's right! Save the $3.40 in your bank account. Decide to buy a generic brand of detergent and deposit the $2.00 savings (cash) in your savings account at the bank. Decide to take your lunch to work one day and deposit the $8.00 you would have spent for lunch with your friends in your savings account in the bank.

All of a sudden you'll see lots of places to save money and you'll watch your savings account grow and grow.

Getting clear about your current beliefs and attitudes about saving your money and your willingness to experiment with saving will be helpful in later chapters when we focus on you and your partner **Building the Family Business**.

Investing and Contributing Your Money

Investing Your Money

What was your family's attitude toward investing? Who do you know who invests? If you could invest in anything you wanted to, what would you invest in?

Do you think only rich people invest?

Successful investors don't invest money, then take it out, then invest in something else and then take it out.

They operate from a plan that's based on their investment goals; how long they have to achieve those goals; their tolerance for risk

57

Couples and Money: Cracking the code to ending the #1 conflict in marriage

(both financial and psychological), and what they can afford to set aside for an investment program.

You want to invest your money according to a plan:

- Set goals based on specific strategies.
- Decide how much you intend to save/earn from your investments over a set period of time.
- Invest on an on-going, consistent basis.
- Don't invest until you're ready.
- Don't buy anything you don't understand.

Contributing Your Money

Some people call it tithing, others refer to it as philanthropy, and still others think of it as just doing their part.

A tithe (from Old English *teogoþa* "tenth") is a one-tenth part of something, paid as a voluntary contribution, usually to support a religious organization.

Philanthropy (from Ancient Greek, meaning "to love people") usually refers to the act of generosity associated with giving money, time, or effort to a charitable cause or institution with the intention of improving the well-being of humanity.

Philanthropy is a major source of income for fine arts and performing arts, religious and humanitarian causes, as well as educational institutions.

A growing trend in philanthropy is the development of *giving circles*, which are small groups of individual donors (very often groups of friends or neighbors), who pool their charitable

58

Values, Attitudes, Beliefs and Habits Related to Managing Money,
Building Wealth and Preventing Conflict

donations and decide together how to use the money to benefit the causes they care about most.

Charitable giving is a term that is more usually used to distinguish non-wealthy people whose individual efforts (donations of time and money to charitable organizations) are, unfortunately, seldom recognized as instigating significant change.

In my opinion, the giving of individuals, no matter how big or small, is no less philanthropic than Bill and Melinda Gates who, as of 2007, were the second-most generous philanthropists in America, having given over $28 billion to charity.

What is your value related to giving your time, energy and money to something outside of yourself for the good of others?

What is your family's value for philanthropy, or tithing, or "doing their part"?

What have you done, specifically, during your life to make the world around you a better place? How did you feel after you did?

What have you taught your children about tithing, philanthropy or charitable giving?

A deeper awareness related to your beliefs and life experience with Investing and Contributing Your Money will be helpful in later chapters when we focus on you and your partner ***Building the Family Business***.

Couples and Money: Cracking the code to ending the #1 conflict in marriage

Building Wealth for Your Future

Wealth is not the same thing as income. Wealth is what you accumulate; not what you earn.

Wealth is NOT measured by what you spend, but rather the opposite. If you earn a lot of money and spend it all on goods and services every year, you're not wealthy. You're living high and being stupid with your money!

That said, whom do you know who makes a lot of money and lives high on the hog, as they say? Do you know anyone who is focused on accumulating money for the long term and is wealthy as a result?

In English-speaking countries we are obsessed with consumerism, buying the latest and greatest technology, the must-have this or that. We sorely lack solid role models, mentors and teachers for building wealth.

The wealthy live a lifestyle that is based on accumulating money. They hold values, embrace attitudes, make decisions and, over time, consistently take actions that forward the accumulation of money for the long-term.

Here are a few behaviors that you can consistently observe in people who build wealth successfully:

- They live in homes and in neighborhoods that are comfortable, but not extravagant. They don't spend huge amounts of money on houses, cars and the trappings of huge financial success.

Values, Attitudes, Beliefs and Habits Related to Managing Money,
Building Wealth and Preventing Conflict

- The wealthy carefully-craft a plan and they stick to it. The wealth-building plan is the priority. They make deliberate decisions about their time, energy and effort related to earning, spending, saving and investing money to ensure their success building wealth.

- They believe that financial fitness and independence is more important than keeping up with the Jones' or living high! Impressing the outside world and social climbing are not part of the plan.

- They make money management a family affair and make it a priority to teach their children about money–earning, spending, saving and investing. They teach their children to respect money and practice wealth-building behaviors. Consequently, their adult children are financially fit and self-sufficient.

True wealth has very little to do with the amount of money you have in the bank. It has everything to do with values, beliefs and attitudes that drive behaviors to accumulate money over the long-term.

"The rich buy assets. The poor only have expenses. The middle class buys liabilities they think are assets. The poor and the middle class work for money. The rich have money work for them."

Robert Kiyosaki

Chapter 6

WAKE UP! YOU AND YOUR PARTNER CAN END MONEY CONFLICTS TOGETHER!

The concept of a healthy couple is morphing into a concept that includes both partners being conscious and emotionally intelligent.

In this chapter we are going to focus on YOU! Who are you as an individual? Who are you as a fully participating partner? What are your legitimate needs and wants? What does it mean to be the full expression of your best and most brilliant passionate Self in the presence of your partner?

As you have more and more Self-knowledge, you will be in a better position to hear from your partner about his/her Self-knowledge. Then, from this aware place, you and your partner can begin to explore your issues related to money and to trust a process that will get you to a peaceful, mutually respectful resolution once and for all!

Wake Up and Be a Conscious Partner!

Being conscious in your relationship means:

- Being Awake;
- Being Present in your connection together;
- Deciding…
  - How you want to be with each other;
  - What you are willing to negotiate;

63

- o   Who you are and what it means to be the full expression of your best Self in the presence of each other;
- Keeping your heart...
  - o   Open;
  - o   Vulnerable;
  - o   Connected to each other!

Become Emotionally Intelligent in Your Relationship!

Becoming emotionally intelligent in your marriage is not an option!

What does it mean to be emotionally intelligent? What are the specific behaviors and attitudes that mean you are emotionally intelligent?

Emotional Intelligence in your relationship is your ability to perceive emotion–yours and your partner's. It is your ability to accurately identify your own emotion; and process information of an emotional nature–yours and your partner's.

When you live with another person on a daily basis you must be able to manage your own emotions, and at the same time be able to accurately identify your partner's emotions in his or her face and voice; and relate to his or her emotions respectfully and lovingly–that is, engage with him or her on an emotional level.

Must-Have Agreements in Your Conscious Relationship

As a conscious partner you understand the importance of making and honoring agreements:

- Your connection to your partner is sacred.

- Something magical happens…you feel connected/truly present together.

- You can always tell when your hearts are open to each other.

- You can tell when she or he shuts you out of his or her heart, and goes unconscious in the relationship.

- You consciously gain mastery of the relationship skills that ensure your success as a happy couple.

- You consciously preserve your connection: you enliven it, deepen it.

- You consciously resolve everything that arises which threatens your relationship together.

Be Aware of What Lies Inside You That Can Threaten Your Love Connection

It is essential to keep in mind that when you fall in love, you surrender your heart and you become very vulnerable. When you are vulnerable you become "hurt-able."

The more you open your heart, the more easily you can be hurt. The more attached you become to your partner (which is completely normal and expected!), the more risk there is.

What's the risk, you ask? The risk is that you lose his or her love or regard; or even your entire relationship!

When you love more and more deeply, there is more risk; and the more the risk, the more there is to lose; and the more there is to

Couples and Money: Cracking the code to ending the #1 conflict in marriage

lose, the more triggered you get. When men and women become triggered, their insecurities skyrocket; their dependency issues emerge with a vengeance; unresolved hurts and unmet needs roll out as though there were no tomorrow.

Relationship Issues Are Opportunities for Your Personal Growth

Recognize that issues that will always emerge in healthy relationships show you the areas where you need to grow and heal as well as that part of your personal work that you are here to do, so you can be fully who you were meant to be!

Understand that it is your job to use the love and safety of your relationship to work on these issues and heal the hurts from the past that keep you stuck. Your issues are valuable opportunities for your personal growth and a deepening connection to your partner.

Communication Break Downs

Think back over the last several years in your current relationship or back to your last relationship.

When you (or your partner) get upset with the other, what happens to your communication?

When tension emerges or tempers flare, how much time does it take for your good communication to dissolve into nothing, or worse?

Wake Up! You and Your Partner Can End Money Conflicts Together!

Who is the blamer in your relationship? There is generally one person who blames the other for the charged issues that are triggered.

Who is on the defensive, defending against being bad or being the problem?

Decide today to be the partner who commits to resolve the obstacles that emerge, and not to let anything interfere with your love and your connection to your partner. Don't let anything be swept under the carpet or go underground; don't leave things unsaid or unresolved.

Learn and Practice Three Main Listening Skills

1. Listening for feelings.
2. Listening to problem-solve.
3. Listening to share thoughts and ideas, receive information and give advice.

There are two separate, but equal parts, to listening: One is the act of hearing and making meaning from the words; the second is the listener's response to the person who is speaking.

Listening is the ability to receive, attend to, interpret and respond appropriately. Effective listening is the ability to respond appropriately to the purpose of the sender.

Couples and Money: Cracking the code to ending the #1 conflict in marriage

The Four Basic Commitments of Conscious Couples

It is very important for these four basic commitments to be an intentional and deliberate part of your conscious relationship structure.

1. I commit to operate in this relationship with good will and with good intention.

2. I am involved and invested in my partner's present and future.

3. I commit to hear and to value my partner's feelings as if they were my own.

4. I commit to engage with my partner until we get to "YES!"

Remember that you are conscious and at choice in your relationship. Instead of saying "Can't" and "No" to your partner, choose to believe that all things are possible; trust that you see your partner accurately and are seen accurately by your partner; know that BOTH of your needs are respected; and agree to start to resolve every disagreement or conflict with H-O-W?

Legitimate Needs and Wants

The plain fact is that we all have needs, and our needs are legitimate.

Needs are those things that are essential to you doing your best, having your best and being your best.

A need can be the desire to have enough clarity, enough money in your bank account, enough invitations to social events or enough recognition or acknowledgement.

Wake Up! You and Your Partner Can End Money Conflicts Together!

It is your personal responsibility to become mindful and to stay mindful of your own needs and wants; as well as the needs and wants of your partner, children and others in your family and social system.

If you are like most people, you are better at keeping track of what others need and want than you are at staying current with yourself and your needs.

- Are you comfortable with the notion that it is your right to have needs and that you cannot meet all your needs yourself?

- Are you clear about some or many of your current needs? Do you recognize your needs and respect them?

- Do you have a good understanding of which needs you can meet and which needs can/must be met by others?

- Do you agree, at least in concept, that it is acceptable and, in fact, reasonable to ask others to meet some of your needs?

- How able and willing are you to honor your needs and to ask others to help you meet your needs?

Personal, individual needs are completely legitimate; and some of your needs must be met by others. You cannot meet all of your needs, nor are you less-than because you cannot. You are simply normal.

A problem (conflict) arises when one or more people have one or more unmet needs or opposing priorities.

"Happiness is not in the mere possession of money; it lies in the joy of achievement, in the thrill of creative effort."

Franklin D. Roosevelt

69

Chapter 7

BUILD THE FAMILY BUSINESS AND HEAD OFF CONFLICTS BEFORE THEY START

The first six chapters of this book have provided solid information that you will begin to pull together and use in this chapter. Now it is time to **Build the Family Business**!

There isn't one right way for you to manage your money and to build wealth. As you have discovered in the first six chapters, your Money Psychology and your personal history, plus your values, beliefs, attitudes and habits (specifically related to earning, spending, accounting for, incurring debt, investing and building wealth) have everything to do with how YOU manage money.

*The nature and structure of the strategies you and your partner employ to build and grow your **Family Business** have everything to do with your success or failure as a couple.*

The best way for you to figure out what will work best for you is to sit down together and to explore all of the possibilities in an open and honest discussion. If the best option doesn't jump out at you, perhaps you should try the one you believe will be the best and see how it works. You can always make adjustments or change your mind completely once you have some experience.

Let's explore the six most common ways to manage money in a marriage.

71

Strategies When One Partner Earns All or Most of the Money:

1. Whole Paycheck System:

Douglas works full time and Denise is a stay-at-home mom. Douglas hands over his paycheck to Denise every month for his wife to manage their money.

Historically, the husband was the wage earner and handed his paycheck over to his wife who was responsible for all household expenditures. This money management system was generally found among lower-income families, where the wife was tasked to stretch inadequate resources to meet the needs of her family. Saving and investing were not part of the structure.

Contemporary couples use this management system differently. Typically today, if the sole or primary earner hands over his or her paycheck to his or her partner, it is because they have decided that she or he is better at maintaining a spending plan, saving, investing and building wealth.

2. Household Allowance:

Peter works full time and Teri is a stay-at-home mom. Peter gives Teri a set amount of money to cover the household expenses. Peter controls the rest of the money. Teri may or many not know how much Peter earns; and she is probably not included in any of the decisions about spending on big-ticket items, about saving and investing or about building wealth.

Strategies When Both Partners Earn Money:

3. Joint Management

Bob and Joan manage their money jointly. They have one joint

Build the Family Business and Head Off Conflicts Before They Start

account so that each of their earnings is deposited in that one "joint" account. Once the money is deposited into the bank, there is no recognition of who has deposited what. All of their expenses are paid out of the joint account; all savings and investments are made from the banked money; all discretionary spending comes out of that account.

4. Individual Management

Ron and Barbara manage their money independently. They do not have a joint account. Each partner has his/her own bank account. They have their own money and are responsible for different shared expenses and make those expenditures accordingly or pool only part of their money for household expenses.

5. Joint + Individual Management—50/50

Tom and Roberta manage their money using the combination approach. They each have their own bank account and they have a joint account. Each partner puts the same amount of money in the joint account and all household expenses get paid out the joint account. Each may do as they please with the balance of their money.

6. Joint + Individual Management—Percentage of Income

Donald and Sue also manage their money using the combination approach. They each have their own bank account and they have a joint account. Each partner deposits the same percentage of his or her income into the joint account (75 percent and 75 percent) vs. the same amount of money ($1,000 and $1,000). All household expenses get paid out of the joint account. Each may do as they please with the balance of their money.

Couples and Money: Cracking the code to ending the #1 conflict in marriage

There is no universal right answer to the question of whether to merge your accounts or to keep them separate. What's most important is to agree on what works for you and to make your money management decisions jointly, as a couple.

Schedule Regular Money Conversations

Make and honor an agreement that you will carve out time regularly to sit down with each other and discuss your finances. Review and track your spending, discuss extraordinary expenses that might be coming up and an approach to paying for them. During this **Money Conversation** make different spending choices when circumstances change; track your savings and debt, and review your investing and wealth building.

Consider ordering a copy of your Credit Report every six months and deciding to create ways to improve your credit score.

If you have credit card debt or other debt, make a plan together to pay it off as quickly as you can. Discuss ways to cut back and support each other to spend less and to put non-essentials on hold until you are debt-free.

Remember that this is a new idea and probably requires new skills, so be patient with yourself and your partner until this becomes more of a routine and begins to feel more comfortable.

Speak with Each Other Respectfully and Responsibly during Money Conversations

Money Conversations can be very emotionally charged. In Chapter 9 we'll focus on the Essential Relationship Success Skills you'll need to learn and practice so as to be able to discuss money easily and effectively.

For now, please understand that it is absolutely essential that you and your partner agree to sit down together, with (1) no personal agenda or desired outcome; (2) an open heart; (3) a very curious attitude; (4) patience; (5) willingness and ability to listen to each other deeply and elegantly; (6) willingness to hear each other's points of view about the best way to reach a mutually acceptable approach; and (7) the desire to manage your money together as a couple.

As in all conversations with your partner, agree to not shout at each other; to not call each other names; to not speak in a mean or degrading way, and to not raise (unresolved) issues from the past.

Support Each Other to Resolve Disagreements about Money

Conflict about money is inevitable. You and your partner have different money histories, money personalities, money psychologies, and different priorities for spending, incurring debt (or not), and for saving, investing and building wealth. Make it your business to learn and practice the Essential Relationship Success Skills that we'll focus on in Chapter 9. These skills will ensure that your **Money Conversations** will be respectful so you can come to a deeper understanding of each other and a way to resolve your differences openly, and settle them equitably.

Money is a microcosm within your relationship. The more you can talk about money, the better your relationship will be.

Your Responsibilities in Your *Family Business*

When Bob and Joan decided to stop handling money in the "old" way and to build their *Family Business*, they scheduled their first **Money Conversation** and spent some time interviewing each other about what they liked and disliked about managing money, and about what each was good at and enjoyed doing or dreaded doing.

At the end of the first **Money Conversation** they decided that Bob would pay the bills, balance the checkbook and file the paperwork; and that Joan would be in charge of the investment accounts. Joan's temperament is much better suited to following the stock market, investigating investment opportunities and checking in with their financial advisors on a regular basis. Bob is more comfortable with the details of day-to-day money management, so it became clear to them that Joan would manage the investment accounts and Bob would manage the money in the household.

The important concept to understand is that regardless of which partner actually sits down to write the checks, balance the checkbook and file the paperwork, or manage the investment accounts, BOTH partners must know what is going on with their household bills and their investments, and BOTH must participate in the final decision-making process together.

How ever you separate the actual tasks, and mutually decide who is going to be responsible to do what, make absolutely certain that you each know and understand what the other is doing.

76

There is no abdicating allowed!

Think of Your Budget as Your Spending Plan

There isn't a successful business on the planet that does not create annual income projections and annual operating budgets. Similarly, these same successful business owners review the monthly income and expenses against the projections to be sure they are on track, and then make adjustments if they are not.

Do you recognize that it makes good sense to apply these sound business principles to your *Family Business*?

When you apply these principles to your *Family Business* you might consider establishing agreements for limits on certain expenses, or maximums you can spend without having to speak with each other. For example, you may agree that neither of you will spend more than $100 a week at the grocery store. If something comes up, you can always agree to spend more one week and cut back the next, or cut back on something else.

Without these guidelines (spending plan or budget) one or both of you might inadvertently spend more than you have, which might ultimately mean not achieving your financial goals.

Creating a household budget makes good sense and is relatively easy to implement. Sticking to it will help you to spend wisely, avoid arguments about how much money to spend and on what, and ensure that you meet your financial goals.

Couples and Money: Cracking the code to ending the #1 conflict in marriage

Set Joint Savings and Retirement Goals

It is important to set joint savings goals. Consider saving money for medical emergencies or unexpected car or appliance repairs; or for a vacation next year, or for a new car or flat- screen TV. Many young families save for the down payment on a house or for their children's education.

Another important reason to save money is for retirement. Retirement might seem very far away today; but the sooner you start saving for retirement, the less you will have to save and the more money you will have when the time comes.

Set Joint Investing Goals and Commit to Wealth-Building Behaviors

It is important to set joint investment goals and to make your money work for you. Investing your money over time can grow into large sums of money later on. If you want to be sure you will have enough money when you retire, give strong consideration to making long-term investments all along the way–even modest investments.

You'll be surprised to see how much you'll earn over the long-term.

Being charitable means different things to different people. For some it can mean giving of yourself, your time and your energy. Volunteering is a powerful way to pay forward kindness and compassion that you have received in your life–or, perhaps, haven't received in your life–and recognize it is the stuff that makes one's life rich and meaningful.

78

For others it can mean contributing financially to a charity or a humanitarian effort. In Judaism, "tzedakah," (a Hebrew word that means "charitable giving") is a family obligation to those who are less fortunate. Giving the "Gift of Tzedakah" can also mean offering help to a total stranger; for example, something as simple as helping an older person cross the street or holding the door open for someone in a wheelchair. According to Jewish law, Jews should give one-tenth of their income to help the poor. Tithing (giving one-tenth of one's income to charity) is part of many religious and spiritual groups.

Do Not Commit Financial Infidelity and Threaten the Integrity of the *Family Business*

Honesty between partners is an essential ingredient for the health and long-term stability of a relationship.

I'm sure you know men and women who go shopping and leave their shopping bags or golf clubs in the car until they can get them into the house without anyone noticing. Then several days or weeks later, they take out those new shoes or that new purse, or that shiny titanium driver; and when their spouses notice that they have something new, they lie and say, "Oh, this old thing! I've had it for years!"

More frequently than you might imagine, husbands and wives will have secret bank accounts or "a stash" of cash someplace in the house that the other partner knows nothing about. Alternatively, one of the partners gets a bonus or a raise, or makes more money overtime than expected, and doesn't disclose it to the other partner; sometimes never disclosing it.

You may have a money management plan similar to that of Tom and Roberta or Donald and Sue (they each have their own bank account and they have a joint account). If you do, it is imperative that during your regularly scheduled **Money Conversations** you make full financial disclosures related to your personal account to each other. This is non-negotiable.

If you were two businesses merging, law would require that both businesses make full financial disclosures. Remember, you have a *Family Business* now!

Teach Your Children about Sound Money Management

Make it a family value and a priority to raise financially aware children.

From the time they are young, talk to them in simple concepts when you are shopping and paying bills; when you are discussing buying a car or a flat-screen TV; when making a charitable donation or considering a volunteer opportunity.

As they get older, hold family **Money Conversations**. Talk about your own philosophies of spending, incurring debt, saving, investing and building wealth.

What does it mean to you? How did your parents handle money? What did they tell you about money? Tell your children stories from your own history and experience with money. These conversations should be short and enjoyable until children get a little older.

You can tie family values and personal values to budgeting and spending decisions; talking about saving and giving goals;

Build the Family Business and Head Off Conflicts Before They Start

exploring volunteer opportunities, or donating their toys to other children less fortunate then they are.

What a perfect time to talk about being thankful! Thankful for personal resources that have nothing to do with money: health, family, skills and talents, and good friends.

As children get older, family money meetings are a great time to talk about how to become savvy consumers and how not to get caught in the quicksand of advertising or peer pressure. It is a great time to discuss their allowance; how to distinguish between a *want* and a *need*, and ways to become an entrepreneur and earn some money to pay for the wants and needs they may have.

It is never too early to start to talk about money with children or, in front of children. Consider giving them money to hand to a sales clerk so they get the feel of money and the chance to connect the dots. Be patient when they make mistakes or make foolish purchases, and be the wise mentor or role model.

In the end, regardless of the nature and structure of the strategies you and your partner employ to build and grow your *Family Business*, remember that managing your money responsibly and respectfully will have everything to do with your success or failure as a couple.

And one last thing: Make your family a **NO ABDICATING ZONE!** Learn to be open and forthcoming! It's worth it!

"No man's fortune can be an end worthy of his being."

Sir Francis Bacon

Chapter 8

YOUR FINANCIAL VISION AND GOALS ARE KEY TO ENDING MONEY CONFLICTS FROM THIS DAY FORWARD

This book is about couples and money. Chapter 8 is a blueprint on how to go inside yourself and figure out what you want the rest of your love life and your financial life to look like, to feel like and to include–in as much detail as possible.

I have developed sixteen Worksheets for this chapter. They are all numbered and they correspond with the subheadings in this chapter.

You can find the Worksheets in the Appendix at the back of the book and online at http://www.crackingthecodebooks.com/couples-money_worksheets.htm. Please download them to your PC or your MAC and print them out and use them as often as you would like.

Let's start at the beginning and explore *YOU*; then move on to explore *You + Your Partner* (as two equal adults), and end with a full exploration of your *US*.

Vision and Goals: A Definition

Vision and Goals are the vehicles we are going to use for this exploration.

Your Vision is a very detailed idea of a desired outcome that you create in your imagination. It is a mental picture of your

83

Couples and Money: Cracking the code to ending the #1 conflict in marriage

desired outcome that includes as many rich details as you can possibly imagine. Your Vision will inspire and energize you to set and achieve goals. Your Vision will also inspire you to choose behaviors that will ensure that the mental picture of an event or a result (desired outcome) that is five to ten years in the future will occur.

Your Goal is a well-defined outcome that gives you clarity, direction, motivation, and focus. Goals are tools that support you to make positive changes in your life. They encourage you to intentionally break old habits and form new habits; and develop a new skill or talent.

My Vision of My Ideal Life

In a perfect world, a relationship is a union of two whole, fully actualized adults. So before you can envision a love-life with your Honey, it makes sense that you will have to have a very strong sense of what your own life will be when you live your best and most brilliant, passionate life!

Use Worksheet #1 to write your Vision Statement. It can be any length you want it to be. Generally it is on the long side because of the detail you include.

Your Vision statement is written in the present tense as if you were reporting what you actually see, hear, think and feel…as if it has already happened and it is your Present. Allow your Vision to open your eyes to all that is possible.

Where do you want to be? Who do you want to be interacting with? What are the essential elements of your life; the Who, the

84

*Your Financial Vision And Goals Are Key To Ending
Money Conflicts From This Day Forward*

What, the Where, the When and the Why.

It is a good idea to review this Vision every year or a bit more often if you like, just to make sure that your Vision statement is still describing the ideal outcome you want for your life.

My Vision for My Ideal Life, Which Includes My Partner

This Vision is still related to *your* life and how you want your life to be with your partner in it. How does having a partner change your Vision in "My Vision for My Ideal Life"?

The best way to approach this version of your Vision is to ask yourself who you are when you are in the best possible relationship you can imagine!

What choices and decisions do you make in your life when someone you love is in y*our* life?

This is NOT "*Our*" life yet.

Have Worksheet #1 beside you and add anything that comes into your mind.

To help you recognize more about *you*, answer the questions on Worksheets #2a and #2b.

Consider your natural abilities, gifts, skills and talents.

What do you need to be your best? We will talk more about Needs in Chapters 9 and 10.

85

Remember, you want to ensure that you are a 100% partner and financial partner in your marriage. This Vision statement will stretch your expectations and aspirations and help you jump out of your comfort zone.

It is a good idea to review this Vision every year (or a bit more often if you like), just to make sure that your Vision statement still describes the ideal outcome you want for your life.

My Partner's Vision of His/Her Ideal Life

You are half of your couple and your partner is the other half. Worksheets #3a, #3b and #3c will provide the opportunities for your partner to do the work you just finished, and give you an opportunity to find out what his or her Vision is of his/her Ideal Life and Ideal Life with you.

This is essential work for your partner to complete so you can move together to Our Vision for Our Marriage as Life and Business Partners. The more solid information you have about yourselves and each other the more able you will be to reach your financial goals and stay financially fit!

Our Vision for Our Life Together

Now, armed with lots of solid information about your Vision for Your Ideal Life and Your Ideal Life with Your Partner, you are ready to create a Vision for "US." In this Vision you temporarily suspend your "I" and write a Vision for your life with your partner. Your "WE" is front and center in this Vision.

Your Financial Vision And Goals Are Key To Ending
Money Conflicts From This Day Forward

Make sure both partners work on this Vision either separately, and then combine all the elements; or you work together.

Worksheet #4 will pose questions meant to spark your deepest knowing and allow your hopes and dreams to bubble up and make themselves known to you.

Our Vision for Our Financial Life

An essential aspect of married life is your financial life! Managing your money with your partner and building wealth are basic fundamental requirements of being a healthy, committed couple.

Money cannot make you happy, but intentional decisions and choices related to money can provide the means of unlimited good for you, your family and for many others throughout the course of your life.

The purpose of creating this Vision (Our Vision for Our Financial Life) is to create a mental picture charged with emotion that can serve to inspire, energize, motivate, and stimulate your creativity for the long-term. Your goals will serve as your guide for your on-going success.

How much money do you need? How does each of you intend to contribute to the *Family Business*? Build wealth?

Worksheet #5 is a Venn Diagram. John Venn lived from 1834 to 1923 in England and popularized the idea of Venn diagrams. As a priest and teacher at Gonville and Caius College of Cambridge, he wrote several books, including two on logic.

87

Couples and Money: Cracking the code to ending the #1 conflict in marriage

Venn diagrams help you describe and compare, for example, the beliefs, attitudes, values, attributes and characteristics of two different people, so that you may visually examine and organize similarities and differences.

When you begin to use Venn diagrams, compare and contrast your beliefs, values and attitudes associated with these six essential money behaviors related to your financial fitness:

1. Earning
2. Spending
3. Accounting For
4. Saving
5. Investing money
6. Building wealth

To create a Venn diagram ask yourself the four questions below. Begin by comparing and contrasting in what ways you and your partner are alike and different regarding earning, and make your way to building wealth. Use a different Venn Diagram for each element related to your financial fitness.

1. *What are the most important beliefs, attitudes and values related to earning money?* Write all your answers on a blank sheet of paper. Write as many responses as you can think of in as much detail as possible.

2. *What beliefs, attitudes and values related to earning money do you and your partner have in common?* These answers go into the blank space where the circles intersect and overlap.

3. *What beliefs, attitudes and values related to earning money do you NOT have in common?* These answers go into the non-intersecting portion of each circle.

Your Financial Vision And Goals Are Key To Ending
Money Conflicts From This Day Forward

4. *How are your beliefs, attitudes and values related to earning money the same or different from your partner's? What, specifically, is similar and different?*

What make Venn diagrams interesting are the overlap areas. It is fairly uncomplicated to identify the two circles in the basic Venn diagram. For our purpose, one circle will represent you and the other will represent your ideal partner.

It is the overlap area that stimulates and inspires your thinking and awareness. It is even more powerful than the circles themselves. Life occurs in the overlap areas. This is where the "truth" lies. Use Venn diagrams to identify or birth your deepest personal truth; about any number of life situations, events or people.

There is no right or wrong way to do this. You can include as much or as little information as you wish. You can take a first pass with a portion of the information and deepen and expand your inquiry later. The most important part of this work is the new awareness of all these factors that impact and affect your relationship with yourself and your partner.

I must emphasize that the overlap areas are more powerful than the circles themselves. The overlap areas are where the truth is to be found.

The areas outside the overlap can be different and divergent. Think of the overlap area as that of the highest compatibility.

Let's try an example Venn diagram to demonstrate how this works for comparing and contrasting beliefs.

89

Here's what we know:

- Barb and John are a married couple.
- Barb holds beliefs for: owning lots of different shoes for all kinds of clothes, buying birthday and holiday presents for everyone, taking two vacations every year, buying an affordable home, not using credit cards, buying a reliable car, paying bills on time.
- John holds beliefs for: owning a few pairs of shoes, being an ardent saver of money, building wealth by investing, buying an affordable home, not using credit cards, buying a reliable car, paying bills on time.

This would be shown in a two-circle Venn Diagram as follows:

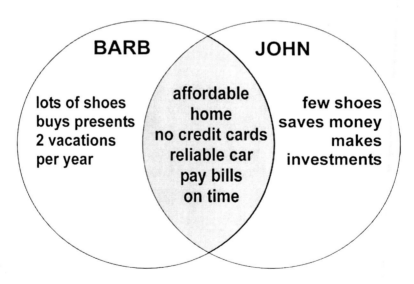

The Barb circle includes her beliefs: lots of shoes, buys presents, two vacations per year

Your Financial Vision And Goals Are Key To Ending
Money Conflicts From This Day Forward

The John circle includes his beliefs: few shoes, saves money, makes investments.

There are no common beliefs that appear in the individual areas of the two circles. The common beliefs are in the overlap area. Both Barb and John hold common beliefs: affordable home, no credit cards, reliable car, pay bills on time.

Our Short-Term Goals

There are three basic kinds of goals:

1. Short-term goals are achievable in under a year.

2. Mid-term goals are achievable in two to five years.

3. Long-term goals are achievable in five-plus years.

You may have multiple goals in one, two or all three time frames; or you may have one specific goal in one, two or in all three time frames. If you have multiple goals, you can certainly work toward them all at once, or concentrate on one and then move to the next.

Your short-term goals are achievable in less than one year.

Worksheet #6a—Personal Goal-Setting Abilities—Our Short-Term Goals will help you and your partner explore the personal resources each of you brings to the short-term goal-setting process, and will help you both recognize where you can contribute the most, and what might get in your way.

Worksheet #6b—Setting the Goals—Our Short-Term Goals will help you and your partner clarify essential aspects of your

91

Couples and Money: Cracking the code to ending the #1 conflict in marriage

short-term goal(s) so you can structure the process for maximum success!

Our Mid-Term Goals

Remember that mid-term goals are achievable in two to five years.

Worksheet #7a—Personal Goal Setting Abilities—Our Mid-Term Goals will help you and your partner explore the personal resources each of you brings to the mid-term goal setting process, and will help you both recognize where you can contribute the most, and what might get in your way.

Worksheet #7b—Setting the Goals—Our Mid-Term Goals will help you and your partner clarify essential aspects of your mid-term goal(s), so you can structure the process for maximum success!

Our Long-Term Goals

And finally, long-term goals are achievable in five-plus years.

Worksheet #8a—Personal Goal-Setting Abilities—Our Long-Term Goals will help you and your partner explore the personal resources each of you brings to the long-term goal-setting process, and will help you both recognize where you can contribute the most, and what might get in your way.

Worksheet #8b—Setting the Goals—Our Long-Term Goals will help you and your partner clarify essential aspects of your long-term goal(s) so you can structure the process for maximum success!

Reminder: This book is intended as a reference only; to educate, inform and entertain. To clarify and structure the short-term, mid-term and long-term goals that will be appropriate for your *Family Business*, please consult a competent professional who specializes in financial planning.

Your Commitments That Support and Forward Your Financial Vision

When you make a commitment to your partner you are making the agreement to be present and available ... physically, mentally and emotionally.

You make agreements by exercising your personal choice. You communicate directly to your partner about what you will do; how you will behave; what she or he can reasonably expect from you, and for what you are willing to be held accountable.

You honor the agreements you make by choosing the behavior that is driven by your values. Your personal values form the set of principles you live by and continually develop as you live your life.

"Principles are like lighthouses—you can either use them to guide you or you can choose to go against them and smash into pieces on the rocks!"

Couples and Money: Cracking the code to ending the #1 conflict in marriage

Being held accountable means you accept responsibility for the results of your choices, decisions and behaviors instead of blaming others or external factors. You believe you are in charge of the quality and direction of your life; that you are NOT a victim of circumstance, and that you are empowered to move forward. You focus on solutions, not problems; and you move forward toward the goals and commitments of your shared vision and purpose, both as individuals and as a couple.

As a conscious couple, you have clarified your personal values, your visions for yourselves as individuals and as a couple, and you have a stronger foundation from which to commit to your agreements and achieve more consistent and satisfying results.

Your overall effectiveness in making and honoring commitments and agreements is greatly increased. Success is an almost certainty when both of you honor your commitments and keep your agreements; and you most certainly are at risk if one person doesn't keep his or her agreements.

Now go back and look at your goals: your short-term, mid-term and long-term goals. Understand that making and honoring commitments is serious business!

Use Worksheet #9 to track the behaviors and develop the commitments that you both believe make sense, and that you both can and will honor so you can make your financial visions, hopes and dreams your financial realities!

"Shoot for the moon! Even if you miss, you'll still be among the stars."

Les Brown

Chapter 9

MASTERING ESSENTIAL RELATIONSHIP SUCCESS SKILLS FOR EFFECTIVE COMMUNICATION MEANS RESOLVING CONFLICTS WITH ONE VOICE

Love is NOT enough!

Successful couples need to be emotionally intelligent; to be conscious; to learn and practice essential relationship skills; and to be courageous, compassionate, committed, tolerant and persistent.

Emotional Intelligence is your ability to perceive emotion; to process information of an emotional nature; to relate to the emotions of another person, to accurately identify your own emotions; to manage your own emotions, and to engage with others on an emotional level

Being a "conscious" couple means being awake, present in your connection together; and deciding h-o-w you want to be with each other; w-h-a-t you are willing to negotiate; w-h-o you are, and what it means to be the full expression of your BEST Self in the presence of each other.

There are highly effective tools and skill-sets that make it possible for you to consciously move through any issue that comes up and to co-create resolution.

In this chapter we are going to focus on the tools and the skill-sets specifically related to communicating effectively with each other about money.

95

Couples and Money: Cracking the code to ending the #1 conflict in marriage

Six Skills for Effectively Resolving Conflicts about Money

There are six basic skills that will enable you and your partner to communicate effectively with each other during a conflict or heated, charged, emotional conversation about money:

1. Accurately identify what you need or want. You do this by asking yourself: *If this situation really worked for me, what would be different?*

2. Find the right words to tell your partner about your needs and wants. This requires that you sit down alone, tell your story to yourself out loud–and over and over–and keep track of the words that keep coming up.

3. Be willing to express what you know to your partner. This means recognizing that nothing changes without talking; and you decide to talk even if it is hard and you are uncomfortable.

4. Communicate from the "I" position. This means you are speaking about yourself, your thoughts and needs, and not speaking about your partner.

5. Listen deeply. This requires that you are curious about what your partner has to say; you are not preoccupied; and you don't think you know how it will end.

6. Be open to the outcome! Resist believing that you won't get your needs met and that no one really cares anyway.

Three Mistakes Couples Make When It Comes to Resolving Conflicts about Money

Conversations about money are almost always charged!

1. The most prevalent mistake is that one or both partners comes to the conversation believing that his or her needs

96

won't be heard, respected, understood, validated or met.

2. One partner doesn't let the other partner finish speaking. He or she interrupts or becomes argumentative about something just said, sometimes well in advance of his or her partner having finished speaking.

3. One or both partners forgets to ensure that it is a good time for both of them to have a conversation to resolve a conflict. Someone forgets to make sure that his or her partner is able and willing to be in listening mode.

Avoiding these common mistakes increases the odds that you will successfully resolve your conflict.

Know What Affects Your Ability to Resolve Conflicts about Money!

Your attitudes and beliefs deeply inform your choices and decisions. They can affirm and esteem you; or, if those attitudes and beliefs are faulty or outdated, they can get in the way and cause you to react versus be proactive on your own behalf. **Negative attitudes, false beliefs and inaccurate judgments affect your ability to effectively resolve conflicts about money.** When you judge, you have generally concluded that the thing that you are judging is either good or bad.

Make sure you come to every conversation with your partner without an agenda, and open to an outcome that honors both of you and meets both of your needs.

Five Steps to Problem-Solve Issues about Money

1. Identify the problem: Whose problem is it? Ask yourself: *Is it mine? Is it yours? Is it ours?*

2. Analyze the problem and gather information. Ask yourself: *What is the problem? How do you know there is a problem? How is it a problem? To whom is it a problem? How does this negatively impact/affect you or your partner? What is the downside (negative aspects) to you or your partner? How do you benefit if the problem is resolved? How does your partner benefit if the problem is resolved?*

3. Generate potential solutions. There are three main tools you can use to generate as many possible solutions as you can think of: Brainstorming, The Five Whys, and The Magic Wand.

    Brainstorming is an activity that you do when you both sit down together and throw out one idea or suggestion after the other, and where no idea is too absurd to consider.

    Asking "why" five times uncovers the basic or fundamental cause of the problem. Clearly articulate the problem. Then one partner asks the other partner "why" five times in succession. Then reverse roles.

    The Magic Wand suspends your reality (stuckness) and elicits your creativity and imagination for your desired outcome.

    Keep track of all the possibilities in writing so you can discuss them at the end of the process.

4. Select and test the solution. The true test of the solution is that the problem is resolved, and that you and your

Mastering Essential Relationship Success Skills For Effective Communication
Means Resolving Conflicts With One Voice

partner are completely satisfied with the outcome. Your needs and your partner's needs are met.

5. Analyze and evaluate the results. Does it make sense for both of you? If neither of you can answer that question with a resounding "yes," go back through the process one more time.

Five Rules of Engagement to Effectively Communicate about Money

The rules of engagement will create an environment for maximum results.

Rule #1: Get Yourself Grounded and in the Right Mind-set

Before you begin the "Five Steps to Problem-Solving," take a deep breath, read through these reminders that will help you get yourself grounded.

Remind yourself that you are not the problem and that your partner is not the problem!

Remind yourself that the problem is that someone's need (or needs) is not being recognized or met. Perhaps you both have needs that are not being recognized or met.

Remind yourself that an acceptable resolution requires that your needs and your partner's needs be met–that no one has given in, given up, or settled for something less than getting important, legitimate needs heard, honored and met.

99

Couples and Money: Cracking the code to ending the #1 conflict in marriage

Rule #2: Self-Esteem Reminder Checklist

From this very grounded place (while you are breathing and centering yourself), go through this "Self-Esteem Reminder Checklist" silently in your mind:

> *"I know myself: my values, beliefs, attitudes and needs. I have self-confidence, and I know that I am good and I am enough. I am willing, responsible and able to create my life to be exactly the way I want it to be.*
>
> *I have gifts, strengths and talents, and they are different from those of others (not less than or better than). I have limitations, and my limitations are about me. They are not about anyone else; and they are not a cause for problems with others. I set appropriate boundaries for myself and not against anyone else."*

Rule #3: Always Engage In a Conversation From The "I" Position

Whenever you have a conversation, speak from the "I" position. Relate what you are saying to yourself and your issues, upsets, frustrations, awareness, thoughts, beliefs, fears, problems, ah-ha moments and so on.

When you share information about yourself to your partner you may say, "As I was listening to you talk about such and such..., I became aware that ...; I flashed on the way ...; I heard my own voice..."

Relating all your reactions, thoughts, feelings and attitudes to yourself will help you to:

100

Mastering Essential Relationship Success Skills For Effective Communication
Means Resolving Conflicts With One Voice

- Stay in integrity;
- Honor yourself and your legitimate needs;
- Become alert to your unrealistic expectations;
- Be aware of the resentment and disappointment you feel;
- Ensure that you communicate effectively and accurately with your partner.

Rule #4: Assess Your Readiness and Your Partner's Readiness to Communicate Effectively

Highly effective communication can only be achieved when BOTH partners are R-E-A-D-Y to communicate.

- Schedule a mutually convenient time to sit down and talk. Be sure to check in with your partner; let him or her know there is a money matter you would like to discuss, and ask when it would be a good time to sit down together and talk.

- When you sit down with each other, be sure you are both in the best and most resourceful personal place inside yourself that you can be in before you begin to speak or listen.

TIP: Take a deep breath. Close your eyes. Take another deep breath. Place your attention inside yourself.

Check for any tension, tightness, hurt feelings, fear, frustration, resentment or disappointment. Now open your eyes. Take a deep breath.

Ask yourself: *Am I in my resourceful, adult part of Self and ready to have this conversation?*

When you know you are ready to speak from this adult, resourceful part of yourself and you are open to listening and hearing, let your partner know. When your partner knows she or he is ready to speak from this adult, resourceful place and is open to listening and hearing, she or he must let you know. When both speaker and listener are ready, you have a Couple's Speaking Contract and may begin.

Rule #5: Speak for the Sole Purpose of Being Known

Never come to the conversation with preconceived ideas or beliefs about what the outcome must be. That limits the possibilities for a positive outcome that could be better than you could have ever imagined.

When you speak with your partner, speak to him or her with the sole purpose of being known. When you listen to your partner, listen for the sole purpose of understanding.

"You must trust yourself more than you trust anyone else with your money."

Suze Orman

Chapter 10

CRAFT ELEGANT AGREEMENTS AND END MONEY CONFLICTS FOREVER!

The purpose of intentionally crafting elegant agreements is that you and your partner accurately reflect who you are, what you are committing to, and agreeing to do and not do.

Most couples have hopes and dreams, desires and expectations. They establish goals and make commitments that are developed from a joint visioning process: a process that expresses an inclusive vision of desired out comes–their road map to success.

The best way to look at this is that we join forces with others by forming agreements.

The Purpose of an Elegant Agreement

Navigating through life and your relationship-life is an ongoing process of creating agreements with each other. An effective agreement means more than getting your partner to do what you want. It means buy-in and true commitment from both people.

Schedule an Intentional Conversation and Co-Create an Elegant Agreement

Agreements are expressed in writing or verbally during very intentional conversations. Most of us have never learned how

103

to craft effective, explicit agreements. It is a skill we were never taught, even though it is fundamental to all relationships and is a basic life skill.

Before You Create an Elegant Agreement

You can use my straightforward 15-Step Process to craft elegant and effective agreements in any kind of relationship, no matter what the nature or structure of the relationship.

All that is required is the willingness of two people to:
- Be mindful of who they are;
- Be honest about what they need or want from the other;
- Act with intention; and
- Follow the Steps exactly!

Dr. Jackie's 15-Step Process to Create an Elegant Agreement

1. Create and clearly articulate your joint vision with as much rich detail as possible. Be sure that both of you participate with eagerness and passion.

2. Be sure that both of you create the agreement with intention and with a belief that you are well-served making and honoring the agreement.

3. Make a list of each person's strengths, gifts, skills and talents that are available to be drawn on by each of you.

4. Be certain that each of you understands and acknowledges the actions (behaviors), attitudes and responsibilities that are associated with the agreement for you and your partner.

Craft Elegant Agreements And End Money Conflicts Forever!

5. Decide together if the actions and attitudes are sufficient to result in the desired outcome(s). If they are not, identify what additional actions and attitudes must be included and by whom.

6. All agreements must include specific time deadlines indicating a time by which each part of the agreement should be completed or finalized. These are "by whens"– by when will you do this, and by when will you do that. In addition, the time period the agreement will be in force must be specified.

7. Does the agreement as a whole and do all the parts of the agreement forward the joint vision?

8. Clearly identify the evidence or positive outcome(s) that you expect to result from each person's making and honoring the agreement.

9. Does the agreement as a whole, and do all the parts of the agreement, truly satisfy each person and result in each person being whole? Being whole refers to being sure that neither person experiences a loss or losses as a result of pledging time, attention and commitment to the agreement.

10. Bring all your concerns and fears to this discussion. This can often minimize the disagreements that may occur during the process of crafting the agreement. This discussion will deepen your commitment to the agreement and to your partner; or reveal a problem that might already be brewing in the relationship.

11. No matter how optimistic and clear you both are when you craft an agreement, one or both of you will likely come back to the table and ask for the agreement to

105

be renegotiated or changed in some way at some time. This is definitely not a personal failure or a failure of the process. **This is an expected, anticipated part of crafting and honoring agreements.**

12. It is critical to include a mechanism that will take into consideration the many changes that normally and naturally occur over time in people's relationships. Being realistic about this at the beginning enables the relationship to evolve and prosper.

13. It is imperative to provide each person with a way to accommodate change–an exit strategy you can both follow with dignity. Anyone who feels imprisoned in an agreement, commitment or relationship will not be his or her best Self or offer all possible personal contributions to forward the joint vision.

14. It is inevitable for conflicts and disagreements to arise and perhaps one of you will not honor the agreement. Establish an attitude of good will and good intention and a plan to repair hurt feelings and disappointments.

15. Both people must be responsible for ensuring that the agreement is honored. Unless and until you are satisfied, do not move into action. Do not agree. Be sure each person is satisfied, is ready to take action and that the outcome will be worth it–then the agreement becomes more of a reality.

Attitudes, Beliefs and Judgments Can Skew the Process

Your attitudes and beliefs deeply inform your choices and decisions. They can affirm and esteem you, or, if those attitudes

Craft Elegant Agreements And End Money Conflicts Forever!

and beliefs are faulty or outdated, they can get in the way and cause you to react rather than be proactive on your own behalf.

When you judge, you have generally concluded that the thing that you are judging is either "good" or "bad."

When you come to the table to resolve an issue, or to craft an elegant agreement, it is essential that you leave your attitudes, beliefs and judgments at the door and allow yourself access to your resourcefulness.

When you are most resourceful, your values drive your behavior. You respect yourself and your partner. You commit to discover an outcome that honors both you and your partner, and both your legitimate needs. You are willing to co-operatively engage in a problem-solving process that will result in an elegant agreement that will affirm and esteem you both; and one that you can honor.

"All riches have their origin in mind. Wealth is in ideas - not money."

Robert Collier

Chapter 11

GRATITUDE STOPS CONFLICT
ONCE AND FOR ALL

There is no limit to what you don't have, and if that is where you put your focus, then your lives will inevitably be filled with endless dissatisfaction.

Most people focus so heavily on the deficiencies in their lives that they barely perceive the good that counterbalances them.

Appreciating and Being Grateful

Getting into the habit of showing appreciation and being grateful affirms you. The things we are lacking are still there; but all of a sudden you will recognize the multitude of goodies you didn't realize were there as well!

Gratitude is NOT Putting on Rose-Colored Glasses

Religions and philosophies have long embraced gratitude as an indispensable manifestation of virtue, and an integral component of health, wholeness and well-being.

There are many examples of how this works. The following example is my favorite:

Roshi John Daido Loori, the spiritual leader and abbot of Zen Mountain Monastery in Mt. Tremper, New York offers...

"Expressing gratitude is transformative, just as transformative as expressing complaint.

Imagine an experiment involving two people. One is asked to spend ten minutes each morning and evening expressing gratitude (there is always something to be grateful for), while the other is asked to spend the same amount of time practicing complaining (there is, after all, always something to complain about).

One of the subjects is saying things like, 'I hate my job. I can't stand this apartment. Why can't I make enough money? My spouse doesn't get along with me. That dog next door never stops barking and I just can't stand this neighborhood.'

The other is saying things like, 'I'm really grateful for the opportunity to work; there are so many people these days who can't even find a job. And I'm definitely grateful for my health. What a gorgeous day. I really like this fall breeze.'

They do this experiment for a year. Guaranteed, at the end of that year the person practicing complaining will have deeply reaffirmed all his negative 'stuff' rather than having let it go, while the one practicing gratitude will be a very grateful person.

Expressing gratitude can, indeed, change our way of seeing ourselves and the world."

Gratitude Stops Conflict Once And For All

Gratitude is a Deliberate, Intentional Behavior

Science is just beginning to catch up as it begins to explore the concept of gratitude. Gratitude is a deliberate, intentional behavior that has inspired many theological and philosophical writings, but it has inspired very little vigorous, empirical research.

We know from tracking personal stories of people who keep gratitude journals on a weekly basis that they exercise more regularly, report fewer physical symptoms, feel better about their lives as a whole, and are more optimistic about the upcoming week compared to those who record hassles or neutral life events.

Those who practice daily gratitude behaviors are more likely to make progress toward important personal goals (academic, interpersonal and health-based) over a two-month period compared to subjects in the other experimental conditions.

Grateful people report higher levels of positive emotions, life satisfaction, vitality, optimism and lower levels of depression and stress. The disposition toward gratitude appears to enhance pleasant feeling states more than it diminishes unpleasant emotions. Grateful people do not deny or ignore the negative aspects of life.

Grateful people are more likely to acknowledge a belief in the interconnectedness of all life and a commitment to and responsibility to others.

People with a strong disposition toward gratitude have the capacity to be empathic and to take the perspective of others.

111

People who practice the principles of gratitude are rated, by their peers and people in their social networks, as more generous and more helpful. They are more likely to help someone with a personal problem or offer emotional support to another.

Grateful individuals place less importance on material goods; they are less likely to judge their own and others' success in terms of possessions accumulated; they are less envious of wealthy people and are more likely to share their possessions with others relative to less grateful people.

Practicing appreciation and gratitude slowly, but insistently, changes your orientation to the world and your life!

Begin YOUR Practice of Gratitude

A simple and effective way to practice gratitude is to integrate giving thanks into your everyday life. In the beginning, it might take you a few minutes or longer to call to mind the people and events for which you are grateful.

Before too long, those people and all the things that happen to you that make you grateful will tumble out of your awareness like an avalanche.

One of the easiest ways to get in the habit of giving thanks and being grateful is to create a gratitude journal. In fact, I recommend you keep a gratitude journal. Date your entries and write daily, weekly or monthly about what you are grateful for, whom you are grateful for, why you are grateful and the events that inspire your gratitude.

Gratitude Stops Conflict Once And For All

Your gratitude journal will become a rich history and the legacy of the valued and cherished moments of your life and life experiences, and the people who helped weave the threads of that rich tapestry.

Three True Stories

When I met Margaret she was deeply in debt and was someone who never missed a sale. Olivia, on the other hand, was someone who would find all kinds of good reasons to not go into a store to buy things for herself or anyone else. Bob was living within his means and was not in debt, and he understood the principles of investing for the long term. While Bob was *doing* everything right, he wasn't including the important element of *being* grateful in his daily life.

None of these three understood the value of the attitude of gratitude or the concept of appreciating or allowing in appreciation.

After a few weeks of keeping their gratitude journals, each one of them began to experience a profound shift in their attitudes and behaviors. They all experienced more energy, clarity, focus and motivation. They all noticed having positive experiences in their lives—everything from unexpected successes at work; improved relationships with colleagues and family members; meeting many more interesting people; resolutions to nagging problems or challenges; and even weight loss and increase in libido!

Why and How to Show Your Appreciation

In Dale Carnegie's *How To Win Friends And Influence People*, one of the most important qualities Carnegie suggested as a

113

Couples and Money: Cracking the code to ending the #1 conflict in marriage

way for people to get along with others is honest and sincere appreciation.

It is so important to show your appreciation. The message that you convey to someone when you show your appreciation is that what they are doing matters to you; and that they matter to you!

Their existence in your memory is indelible!

Your appreciation must be honest and sincere or otherwise you should not communicate it.

When you don't show appreciation, the message is that you don't care what she or he is doing, and you are basically delivering the message that what she or he is doing doesn't matter all that much to you; because if it did matter, you'd notice it, and show your appreciation.

Showing appreciation doesn't have to be some grand gesture. On the contrary, showing your appreciation conveys the message to your partner or to anyone in your life that you appreciate something they did for you, or something about them you value or were touched or tickled by.

Usually, just saying it sincerely is sufficient to convey the message.

Want to practice? Go ahead and thank your partner for something she or he did today or yesterday. Find something that matters to you and convey your appreciation.

It costs you so little and it means so much to others!

114

Gratitude Stops Conflict Once And For All

Showing Others Appreciation is One Side of the Coin

How many times has someone said something nice to you–appreciating an action or something you did, acknowledging your work, your appearance or your mental ability–and you've responded: "Oh, it was nothing really," or "No, really, it's just the color of this suit," or "Anybody could have done it"?

What you are saying to them is "You're wrong!" You are telling them that their appreciation is in error and that they have made a mistake. How do you think that makes them feel? The flip side of the appreciation coin is your ability to accept appreciation when others convey their appreciation to YOU!

When you actually verbalize your gratitude or appreciation you don't want someone to say "You are wrong." You hope that it will make them feel *good*, not embarrassed! With that in mind, when someone offers you their appreciation, accept it gracefully. All you need to say is "Thank you!"

Create a Gratitude Journal

Find one thing to be grateful for each day–you will be surprised how quickly you will have a whole list! And how fast you will want to remind yourself about all the things you are grateful for.

Gratitude can't co-exist with arrogance, resentment and selfishness. Stop taking for granted the many precious and wonderful aspects of your life. Begin each day with a moment of gratitude, perhaps for even just waking up and being able to get out of bed; or for looking out of your window to see another day full of possibility; or for having one more day to enjoy. Be amazed and be involved in life.

115

Couples and Money: Cracking the code to ending the #1 conflict in marriage

Whenever you learn anything new, the most important part is to operationalize it! That means that you will actually be able to use the learning and to make a quantifiable and sustainable change in your life: in this case, a change around money.

You must create a structure for whatever you learn and come to know and believe, so you can use this new knowing and understanding easily and effortlessly. Nothing should get in the way of your success utilizing the new knowing and learning.

In order to make these skills, tools and strategies available to you, you'll need to be aware of the things that may stop you.

What is generally meant by resistance and self-sabotage is that even though some part of you is excited about embracing a change or a shift in an attitude or behavior, another part of you isn't interested in anything new and puts on the brakes.

- Can you think of a time in your life when a part of you tried to behave in a new way or tried to change an old behavior? What happened?
- What experience(s) do you remember having?
- Did you hear or sense the voice(s) of caution or resistance that may have been present?
- What, if anything, kept you or stopped you from moving forward and making this change?
- Did a part of you try to limit your interest or willingness to explore and try new things?
- Did a part of you try to restrict or rein in your enthusiasm and eagerness?
- Did a part of you successfully keep you from changing old behaviors and attitudes, even though you really wanted to?

116

Gratitude Stops Conflict Once And For All

Be true to yourself and remember that you deserve to have the financial life and the relationship with money that you and your partner want to have. Don't allow others or a part of yourself to deprive you of what is rightfully yours.

Commit to Making Changes Specifically Related to Earning, Spending, Accounting for, Saving, and Investing Money Consciously and with Purpose

There are many voices inside you. Whenever you consider doing anything that is unfamiliar or unknown, one or more of your voices gets triggered or activated. That translates into behavior that can look like caution or resistance.

Understand that changing anything in your life happens slowly. Make a commitment to the change you want to make: consciously, intentionally, and deliberately. Identify the specific decisions and behaviors that are required to make the change and to make it sustainable.

This will help you to deal with the voices inside you that are encouraging you to abandon the attempt to change. Each positive step towards achieving the desired change will lessen the power of the inner voices.

"You have not lived a perfect day, even though you have earned your money, unless you have done something for someone who will never be able to repay you."

Ruth Smeltzer

Chapter 12

AVOID THE NEGATIVE IMPACT OF ADHD ON YOU AND YOUR FAMILY BUSINESS

Managing your *Family Business* is a unique challenge for people with ADHD. The people around you and your financial fitness are severely impacted by procrastination, disorganization, and impulsive acts.

While there is no published research directly relating financial issues and ADHD in adulthood, Chapter 12 will (1) identify the major problem areas with money for adults with ADHD; (2) explore specific behaviors commonly related to adults with ADHD; (3) review specific relationship success skills related to earning, spending, not creating debt, saving, investing and building wealth; and (4) create some practical solutions to resolve the problems.

Your Problem Areas with Money

Most people with money problems believe that not having enough money is by far their biggest problem.

Adults with ADHD are no different, and are also generally unable to identify any of the specific money behaviors that result in being financially fit–or not.

If you are an adult with ADHD, there are some common "money behaviors" that you may struggle with:

- You do not earn *enough* money (financial underachieving).

119

Couples and Money: Cracking the code to ending the #1 conflict in marriage

- You do not have a Spending Plan.

- You forget when the car payment or mortgage is due.

- You procrastinate paying monthly bills.

- You lose or do not pay monthly bills at all.

- You are not organized with papers.

- You do not keep track of checkbook balances.

- You lose checks.

- You bounce checks.

- You spend impulsively–buy things on a whim.

- You do not have a Saving Plan.

- You do not save for the future or for possible emergencies (car/appliance repairs; retirement).

- You do not save for big-ticket items (vacations, children's college).

- You carry large credit card balances.

- You do not have a plan to get out of debt and stay out of debt.

- You do not have an Investment Plan.

- You do not have a long-term Wealth-building Plan.

If you are an adult with ADHD there are three *good* reasons why managing money might be especially challenging for you:

1. You have so many choices related to spending and managing money. The decisions you need to make can become overwhelming, added to the fact that adults with ADHD prefer to avoid making decisions when they can.

2. The whole idea of money is not easy to visualize. Adults with ADHD generally do better with concepts and ideas they can visualize.

120

3. Day-to-day management of the *Family Business* isn't fun and exciting. I might even go so far to say that it can be boring and tedious. Adults with ADHD have a much easier time when tasks are interesting and stimulating.

Your Vision for Your Life and Your *Family Business*

When it comes to money management and the *Family Business*, vision is one of the key elements, but watch out for becoming too focused.

Many adults with ADHD can become too focused on creating a vision, and can obsess on creating the perfect budget, or optimizing the perfect savings plan or the perfect investment portfolio. Be careful and be sure to connect the reality of your money behavior to the elements in your vision. If your vision doesn't include some fun behaviors, your likelihood for success is limited.

Be sure to use the Worksheets #1 through #5 in Chapter 8 frequently!

Your Goals and Your *Family Business*

Remember our discussion in Chapter 8 about goals? A goal is a well-defined outcome that gives you clarity, direction, motivation and focus. Goals are tools that support you to make positive changes in your life. They encourage you to intentionally break old habits and form new habits; and develop a new skill or talent.

We also said that there are three kinds of goals: Short-term, mid-term and long-term goals.

Couples and Money: Cracking the code to ending the #1 conflict in marriage

While setting goals for adults with ADHD can be highly problematic, it is also very possible if you know what to watch out for and then put solid strategies in place:

- You have too many goals and procrastination sets in.
- You underestimate the time you need and the steps that must be included to complete your goal.
- You often forget to consider if your goal is measurable, reasonable and achievable.
- You often neglect to create a reasonable and achievable time frame to complete your goal.
- You often neglect to breakdown a long-term goal into a number of reasonable, achievable short-term and mid-term goals.
- You forget to review and revise your goals every once in a while.

Please make sure your goals reflect the changes you want to create in your life. Goals must be measurable, reasonable and achievable. Goals are not etched in concrete. Don't hesitate to abandon any goal the minute you decide–mindfully and intentionally–that the goal no longer matches the change you want to make in your life.

In addition to setting goals, planning and consistency are often very challenging money behaviors for adults with ADHD. Putting structures and systems in place will help you to be more consistent. Resist the temptation to focus on creating perfect plans and systems, rather than creating realistic ones.

Adults with ADHD retain information better when it is presented in a visual format. So, remember to use all the Worksheets #6a

122

through #8b in Chapter 8 to keep very close track of your goal setting and your progress.

Shop 'Till You Drop

Impulsivity, one of the hallmarks of ADHD, can lead to financial difficulties. Impulsive shopping and spending is defined as any purchase you did not plan to make when you left the house that morning, any purchase that is not a part of your budget, or any purchase that you don't need. For an adult with ADHD, this spending happens spontaneously and without warning.

Once in a while everyone spends money to feel better. Many adults with ADHD spend money to indulge themselves frequently and excessively; more commonly making lots of small purchases to make them feel good vs. making one lavish purchase.

Emotional spending (and usually creating debt) includes retail shopping, health and beauty treatments, eating out, gambling and entertainment.

Here are a few reasons adults with ADHD over spend:

- You soothe yourself after a bad day or to reward yourself for a good one.
- You cope with work or relationship stress.
- You diffuse your feelings of anger or frustration.
- You get bored easily.

Reach Out and Find Support

It is possible for adults with ADHD to stop out-of-control spending and become tremendously successful money managers. The three behaviors that will help you be successful are (1) planning; (2) creating routines; and (3) developing trusted support systems (including specifically identified people).

Successful money management and financial fitness require your attention, your deliberate intention, and a whole host of choices and behaviors on a daily basis.

When adults with ADHD use the tools and strategies included in this book they will improve their money management skills, and be more easily able to build and maintain a financially sound *Family Business*.

"The art of living lies less in eliminating our troubles than in growing with them."

Bernard M. Baruch

Suggested Resource for Adults with ADHD:
Shane K. Perrault, Ph.D.
ADHD Performance Clinic
1400 Spring St., Ste 370
Silver Spring, MD, USA 20910
301.588.4600
www.ADHDpc.com

EPILOGUE

Your Final Thoughts

In any change process there are always parts of Self that will resist the change even when 99.9999% of Self wants the change(s) and can recognize the huge benefits of the change(s).

Before you put this book down, take a moment and answer these questions in as much depth and detail as possible and with as much honesty as you can:

I invite you to really try to answer all these important questions in as much depth as possible and with as much honesty as you can. Use your very last Worksheet #10–Final Thoughts–to record your current thoughts and new awareness.

- What was the best idea, piece of new information or point of view you have learned from this book?

- What information or point of view evoked the most emotion? Note: your emotion can be excitement, curiosity, fear, apprehension, etc.

- What thoughts did you notice as you were reading the information and answering the questions throughout the book?

- What thoughts or points of view did you disagree with? Which offended you?

- What might keep you from moving forward and using the information presented in this book? Why?

- If you allow change(s) to become part of your life right now, what might you lose?

- If you allow change(s) to become part of your life right now, how will you have to think of yourself?

- If you allow change(s) to become part of your life right now, what perceptions or beliefs about you will have to change?

- If you allow change(s) to become part of your life right now, how might others think of you?

- Specifically, which question, piece of information or suggestion required you to stretch beyond your comfort zone?

Remember ...

... for most humans, change is a slow process. Please know and trust that you are engaging in a serious change process just because you were interested enough to purchase this book. We all change and grow in different ways and at varying rates of speed. Keep showing up for YOU in your life, and you'll get where you are going.

Thank you for permitting me to stretch you and to offer some thoughts and ideas for your careful consideration! I wish you every success on this life-long journey of making your life and your love life extraordinary and joyful!

Epilogue

There is an old Chinese proverb:

> *"All roads lead to the same summit.*
> *It is not where you are going;*
> *it is about the journey."*

Good luck!
Remember, only YOU can make it happen!

APPENDIX

A B-o-n-u-s from Dr. Jackie!

All the Worksheets for Chapter 8 and the Epilogue are printed here, and are online for you! All you have to do is visit the Cracking the Code Book Series website, download the Worksheets to your computer and print them out at your convenience so you can use them any time and as often as you want.

http://www.crackingthecodebooks.com/couples-money_worksheets.htm

Couples and Money: Cracking the code to ending the #1 conflict in marriage

Worksheet 1
My Vision of My Ideal Life

If you could wave a magic wand and create a life that includes anything and everything you ever wanted, what would your life include?

_____

_____

_____

_____

_____

_____

_____

_____

If you could imagine your life (your personal world) exactly as you want it to be, how would it be?

_____

_____

_____

_____

_____

_____

_____

_____

Appendix - Worksheets

What activities do you love to do? What have you made a part of your life for as long as you can remember?

_____

_____

_____

_____

What energizes you?

_____

_____

_____

_____

What fills you with pride?

_____

_____

_____

_____

What experiences warm your heart and touch your spirit?

_____

_____

_____

_____

Couples and Money: Cracking the code to ending the #1 conflict in marriage

Worksheet 2a
My Vision for My Ideal Life, Which Includes My Partner

Now you can deepen your Vision of your ideal life and include your partner in your Vision. Take a moment and think about your life. Ask yourself these questions:

What are five things I can do this week to create my best and most brilliant passionate life with my partner? These don't have to be huge things—indeed, they can be quite small—as long as they take you in the direction you want to go.

1. _____

2. _____

3. _____

4. _____

5. _____

What are my natural abilities, talents and skills that are my strengths and assets? You should know this—but it's always worth asking one or two people you really trust what they think you are particularly good at. You may be surprised at the answer! We often take our own talents for granted.

Appendix - Worksheets

What is it about me that others most value? Think of the things that people say about you. This isn't the time for being modest–be proud of what you offer to others.

_____

_____

_____

_____

_____

_____

_____

_____

Do you have a sense or a glimpse of your vision? _____

Looking back over your life, can you notice any specific behaviors, decisions or choices you made or didn't make, or wish you had made? What kind of driver have you been, thus far, in your vehicle of life?

_____

_____

_____

_____

Couples and Money: Cracking the code to ending the #1 conflict in marriage

Appendix - Worksheets

Worksheet 2b

My Vision for My Ideal Life, Which Includes My Partner

Most of us are better at keeping track of what others need and want, rather than keeping track of our own needs and ourselves. By answering the following questions, you will find it easier to identify where you may need to do some work.

	Yes/No
Are you comfortable with the notion that it is your right to have needs, and that you cannot meet them all?	
Are you clear about some or many of your current needs? Do you recognize your needs and respect them?	
Do you have a good understanding of which needs you can meet by yourself and those which must be met by others?	
Are you comfortable with the idea that some of your needs MUST be met by other people?	
Do you agree, at least in concept, that it is acceptable and, in fact, reasonable to ask others to meet some of your needs?	
Are you able and willing to honor your needs and ask others to help you meet your needs?	

If you did not answer YES to all of these questions, don't despair; we'll be looking at this more closely later.

135

Couples and Money: Cracking the code to ending the #1 conflict in marriage

Worksheet 3a
My Partner's Vision of His/Her Ideal Life

If you could wave a magic wand and create a life that includes anything and everything you ever wanted, what would your life include?

_____

_____

_____

_____

_____

_____

_____

If you could imagine your life (your personal world) exactly as you want it to be, how would it be?

_____

_____

_____

_____

_____

_____

_____

Appendix - Worksheets

What activities do you love to do? What have you made a part of your life for as long as you can remember?

_____

_____

_____

_____

What energizes you?

_____

_____

_____

_____

What fills you with pride?

_____

_____

_____

_____

What experiences warm your heart and touch your spirit?

_____

_____

_____

_____

Couples and Money: Cracking the code to ending the #1 conflict in marriage

What things must be part of your world so that you can be your best Self?

_____

_____

_____

_____

_____

_____

_____

_____

_____

_____

_____

Appendix - Worksheets

Worksheet 3b
My Partner's Vision of His/Her Ideal Life Including Me

Now you can deepen your Vision of your ideal life and include your partner in your Vision. Take a moment and think about your life. Ask yourself these questions:

What are five things I can do this week to create my best and most brilliant passionate life with my partner? These don't have to be huge things—indeed, they can be quite small—as long as they take you in the direction you want to go.

1. _____

2. _____

3. _____

4. _____

5. _____

What are my natural abilities, talents and skills that are my strengths and assets? You should know this—but it's always worth asking one or two people you really trust what they think you are particularly good at. You may be surprised at the answer! We often take our own talents for granted.

139

What is it about me that others most value? Think of the things that people say about you. This isn't the time for being modest–be proud of what you offer to others.

_____

_____

_____

_____

_____

_____

_____

_____

Do you have a sense or a glimpse of your Vision? _____

Looking back over your life, can you notice any specific behaviors, decisions or choices you made or didn't make, or wish you had made? What kind of driver have you been, thus far, in your vehicle of life?

_____

_____

_____

_____

_____

_____

Appendix - Worksheets

Couples and Money: Cracking the code to ending the #1 conflict in marriage

Worksheet 3c
My Partner's Vision of His/Her Ideal Life Including Me

Most of us are better at keeping track of what others need and want, rather than keeping track of our own needs and ourselves. By answering the following questions, you will find it easier to identify where you may need to do some work.

	Yes/No
Are you comfortable with the notion that it is your right to have needs and that you cannot meet them all?	
Are you clear about some or many of your current needs? Do you recognize your needs and respect them?	
Do you have a good understanding of which needs you can meet by yourself and those which must be met by others?	
Are you comfortable with the idea that some of your needs MUST be met by other people?	
Do you agree, at least in concept, that it is acceptable and, in fact, reasonable to ask others to meet some of your needs?	
Are you able and willing to honor your needs and ask others to help you meet your needs?	

If you did not answer YES to all of these questions, don't despair; we'll be looking at this more closely later

Appendix - Worksheets

Worksheet 4
Our Vision of Our Life Together

Spend some quiet, quality time with your partner, and together craft a Vision of your life together as "WE." Let yourselves daydream for an hour or two and create an image of your life together. Include anything and everything you ever wanted. What would your life include?

Use as much detail as possible. Don't limit yourself; all things are possible; and don't let your fears get in the way. Don't worry about how realistic or unrealistic your Vision seems to be: let your imagination take over!

When you think of your life as "WE," think of your personal world of family and friends, your home and children, your extended families. This includes everything in the world that touches you in some way every day and how you want that to be.

_____

_____

_____

_____

_____

_____

_____

_____

_____

Couples and Money: Cracking the code to ending the #1 conflict in marriage

_____

_____

_____

_____

_____

_____

What is your life like living with each other? If you could imagine your life (your personal world) exactly as you want it to be with him or her, how would it be?

_____

_____

_____

_____

What activities do you love to do? How do you express and share that with each other?

_____

_____

_____

_____

144

Appendix - Worksheets

What energizes you? How do you express and share that with each other?

_____

_____

_____

_____

What fills you with pride? How do you express and share that with each other?

_____

_____

_____

_____

What experiences warm your heart and touch your spirit? How do you express and share that with each other?

_____

_____

_____

_____

Couples and Money: Cracking the code to ending the #1 conflict in marriage

What things must be part of your world so that you can be your best Self in the presence of each other?

_____

_____

_____

_____

How will you include or integrate someone else into those parts of your world? Or do you? If you don't, what kinds of boundaries do you establish? How able are you to set and maintain your boundaries (that is, asking for what you need and want)?

_____

_____

_____

_____

What personality and character traits (yours and your ideal partner's) must be present? What are acceptable or tolerable? What are non-negotiable or unacceptable? Which ones must be present?

_____

_____

_____

_____

Appendix - Worksheets

Worksheet 5
Our Vision of Our Financial Life

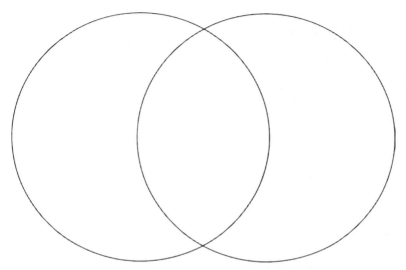

Compare and contrast your values, beliefs and attitudes in these essential components of your financial life with the values, beliefs and attitudes of your partner:

Earning Money	Spending	Accounting for Money	Saving
Incurring Debt	Investing	Building Wealth	Other

147

Couples and Money: Cracking the code to ending the #1 conflict in marriage

Worksheet 6a
Our Short-term Goals—Personal Goal-Setting Abilities

Strengths: _____

_____

_____

_____

Gifts: _____

_____

_____

_____

Skills: _____

_____

_____

_____

Talents: _____

_____

_____

_____

Abilities: _____

_____

_____

_____

Appendix - Worksheets

Strong Preferences: _____

_____

_____

_____

Willingness: _____

_____

_____

_____

Non-negotiable (what I hate to do and won't do): _____

_____

_____

_____

Couples and Money: Cracking the code to ending the #1 conflict in marriage

Worksheet 6b
Our Short-term Goals—Setting the Goals

What is the goal? _____

_____

_____

_____

What are the relevant steps to achieving this goal (actions)?

_____

_____

_____

_____

What is the timeframe for each action? _____

_____

_____

_____

Why is this goal important to ME?_____

_____

_____

_____

150

Appendix - Worksheets

Why is this goal important to US?_____

_____

_____

_____

What are the potential roadblocks that might get in our way?

_____

_____

_____

_____

What are the strategies we can use to overcome the roadblocks?

_____

_____

_____

_____

What are the positive benefits to achieving this goal?

_____

_____

_____

_____

Couples and Money: Cracking the code to ending the #1 conflict in marriage

What are the negative consequences in not achieving this goal?

_____

_____

_____

_____

Appendix - Worksheets

Worksheet 7a
Our Mid-term Goals—Personal Goal-Setting Abilities

Strengths: _____

_____

_____

_____

_____

Gifts: _____

_____

_____

_____

_____

Skills: _____

_____

_____

_____

_____

Talents: _____

_____

_____

_____

_____

Couples and Money: Cracking the code to ending the #1 conflict in marriage

Abilities: _____

_____

_____

_____

Strong Preferences: _____

_____

_____

_____

Willingness: _____

_____

_____

_____

Non-negotiable (what I hate to do and won't do): _____

_____

_____

_____

_____

Appendix - Worksheets

Worksheet 7b
Our Mid-term Goals—Setting the Goals

What is the goal? _____

_____

_____

_____

_____

What are the relevant steps to achieving this goal (actions)? ____

_____

_____

_____

_____

What is the timeframe for each action? _____

_____

_____

_____

_____

Why is this goal important to ME?_____

_____

_____

_____

_____

155

Couples and Money: Cracking the code to ending the #1 conflict in marriage

Why is this goal important to US?_____

_____

_____

_____

_____

What are the potential roadblocks that might get in our way?

_____

_____

_____

_____

What are the strategies we can use to overcome the roadblocks?

_____

_____

_____

_____

What are the positive benefits to achieving this goal? _____

_____

_____

_____

_____

Appendix - Worksheets

What are the negative consequences in *not* achieving this goal?

_____

_____

_____

_____

Couples and Money: Cracking the code to ending the #1 conflict in marriage

Worksheet 8a
Our Long-term Goals—Personal Goal-Setting Abilities

Strengths: _____

_____

_____

_____

_____

Gifts: _____

_____

_____

_____

_____

Skills: _____

_____

_____

_____

_____

Talents: _____

_____

_____

_____

_____

Appendix - Worksheets

Abilities: _____

_____

_____

_____

_____

Strong preferences: _____

_____

_____

_____

_____

Willingness: _____

_____

_____

_____

_____

Non-negotiable (what I hate to do and won't do): _____

_____

_____

_____

_____

Couples and Money: Cracking the code to ending the #1 conflict in marriage

Worksheet 8b
Our Long-term Goals—Setting the Goals

What is the goal? _____

_____

_____

_____

_____

What are the relevant steps to achieving this goal (actions)?

_____

_____

_____

_____

What is the timeframe for each action? _____

_____

_____

_____

_____

Why is this goal important to ME?_____

_____

_____

_____

_____

Appendix - Worksheets

Why is this goal important to US?_____

_____

_____

_____

_____

What are the potential roadblocks that might get in our way?

_____

_____

_____

_____

What are the strategies we can use to overcome the roadblocks?

_____

_____

_____

_____

What are the positive benefits to achieving this goal? _____

_____

_____

_____

_____

Couples and Money: Cracking the code to ending the #1 conflict in marriage

What are the negative consequences in *not* achieving this goal?

_____

_____

_____

_____

Appendix - Worksheets

Worksheet 9

Our Commitments that will Make Our Financial Vision a Reality

Partner A	Partner B
_____	_____

Couples and Money: Cracking the code to ending the #1 conflict in marriage

Worksheet 10
Your Final Thoughts

Answer these questions in as much depth as possible and with as much honesty as you can:

What was the best idea, piece of new information or point of view you have learned from this book?

_____

_____

_____

_____

What information or point of view evoked the most emotion? Note: your emotion can be excitement, curiosity, fear, apprehension, etc.

_____

_____

_____

_____

What thoughts did you notice as you were reading the information and answering the questions throughout the book?

_____

_____

_____

_____

Appendix - Worksheets

What thoughts or points of view did you disagree with? Which offended you?

_____

_____

_____

_____

Specifically, which question, piece of information or suggestion required you to stretch beyond your comfort zone?

_____

_____

_____

_____

What might keep you from moving forward and using the information presented in this book? Why?

_____

_____

_____

_____

If you allow change(s) to become part of your life right now, what might you lose?

_____

_____

_____

Couples and Money: Cracking the code to ending the #1 conflict in marriage

If you allow change(s) to become part of your life right now, how will you have to think of yourself?

What perceptions or beliefs about you will have to change?

If you allow change(s) to become part of your life right now, how might others think of you?

GLOSSARY OF TERMS

Accounting For Your Money; Money Management
The process of knowing where you are spending your money today, and having a well- thought-out plan in place for where you want it to go in the future.

Asking "WHY"
A problem-solving technique that includes asking "why" five times, which results in uncovering the basic or fundamental cause of the problem.

Assets
Your personal assets may include your creativity, curiosity, energy and your passion–the activities that bring you great energy, as well as your unique strengths and natural talents, which includes the set of proven skills and abilities at which you are very, very good.

Attitudes
Your attitudes are aligned with your values and, at the same time, are much more flexible than your values. Attitudes are generally defined as a way of looking at life; a way of thinking, feeling and behaving. Attitude is your feelings or mood toward people, events and circumstances.

Being Whole
In relationships, the nature and structure of conversations, commitments, and agreements includes the **absolute** requirement that neither partner experiences a loss or losses as a result of his or her participation, commitment or agreement to something that benefits both partners.

167

Couples and Money: Cracking the code to ending the #1 conflict in marriage

Beliefs

Any cognitive content that a person holds as true regarding people, concepts, or things, including themselves, are beliefs. Your early life experiences serve to deeply inform your beliefs about who you are, how the world works, and what your place is in it. Your beliefs shape your expectations; assumptions; what you think you are capable of; impel you to interact with the world in a particular way or not; and, accordingly, create your experience of life and the world around you.

Best Self

When you are acting with deliberate intention and with the highest integrity; being respectful of yourself and of others; honoring yourself and others, and staying mindful and appreciative of your unique skills and talents, only then are you being your Best Self!

Brainstorming

A problem-solving technique that includes both partners sitting down together and throwing out one idea or suggestion after the other, and where no idea is too "way out" or absurd to consider.

Budgeting

An approach to keep track of all financial details. Budgeting involves understanding how much money you earn and spend over a period of time. When you create a budget, you are creating a plan for spending and saving money.

Charitable Giving

A term that is usually used to distinguish the individual efforts (donations of time and money to charitable organizations) by non-wealthy people.

168

Glossary Of Terms

Couples Speaking Contract

Highly effective communication can only be achieved when both partners are ready to communicate (that is, one is ready to speak and the other is ready to listen). Prior to beginning a conversation, it is essential that partners check in with themselves and ensure that they are (1) in the resourceful, adult part of Self; (2) open to speaking or listening and hearing; and (3) ready to have a conversation. When both partners are ready, you have a Couple's Speaking Contract.

Elegant Agreement

An agreement is commonly defined as "a mutual understanding between two or more individuals." An Elegant Agreement relates to a joint Vision that is clearly articulated by both partners. Each individual enters into the agreement with a personal commitment to ensure that the *other* person's interests, needs and desired outcome(s) are taken in account and met, in addition to their own interests, needs and desired outcome(s) being met. All the parts of an Elegant Agreement truly satisfy each person and result in each person being whole.

Emotional Intelligence

EI in your relationship is your ability to perceive emotion—yours and your partner's. It is your ability to accurately identify your own emotion; and to process information of an emotional nature —yours and your partner's.

Habit

A pattern of behavior that occurs automatically. Habits are routines of behavior that are repeated regularly, and occur subconsciously without directly thinking, or deciding or being intentional about them.

169

Hoarders

Men and women who can't part with their money; who fiercely fight against spending money on themselves or others for any reason.

"I" Position

This means you are speaking about yourself, your thoughts and needs; and not speaking about your partner or any other person.

Listen Deeply

This requires that you are curious about what your partner has to say; you are not preoccupied; and you don't think you know how it will end.

Magic Wand

A problem-solving technique that suspends your reality (stuckness) and elicits your creativity and imagination for your desired outcome.

Money Scripts

Your beliefs about money that reside in your unconscious mind and guide your every decision, and inform your every behavior related to money, and buying goods and services.

Needs

Those things that are essential to you doing your best, having your best and being your best. A need can be for enough clarity, enough money in your bank account, invitations to social events or enough recognition or acknowledgement.

Over Spenders

Men and women overspend because possessions give them identity. They believe that they will be happy and life will be everything they ever hoped and dreamed it would be IF they just had… (fill in the blank).

Philanthropy

Philanthropy (from Ancient Greek, meaning "to love people") usually refers to the act of generosity associated with giving money, time, or effort to a charitable cause or institution with the intention of improving the well-being of humanity.

Poverty Thinking or Scarcity Scripting

If you have a basic, fundamental attitude that people and events outside you can't be trusted, or your thinking process is rooted in fear versus all things are possible all the time, you are operating from an internal base known as Poverty Thinking or Scarcity Scripting.

Prosperity Thinking or Abundance Scripting

If you have a basic, fundamental attitude that at the end of the day you k-n-o-w that "things will work out" you are operating from an internal base known as Prosperity Thinking.

Spenders or Amassers

Men and women who have created enormous wealth and spend money for the pure joy of spending, and the love of owning beautiful clothes, art, jewels, traveling, and the like.

Tithe

A tithe (from Old English *teogoþa* "tenth") is a one-tenth part of something, paid as a voluntary contribution, usually to support a religious organization.

Under Spenders

Men and women who resist spending even when it will result in dire consequences for themselves or others in their lives.

Values

Your values are formed directly from your early beliefs, which are formed by your early life experiences. Your values reflect the people, places, things and concepts that you believe are most important; and without which you cannot be your best and most brilliant, passionate Self! Your values are deeply held personal beliefs about what you regard as important, worthy, desirable or right.

Wealth

Wealth is what you accumulate, not what you earn. The wealthy or the affluent (as they are sometime referred to), live a lifestyle that is based on accumulating money. They hold values, embrace attitudes, make decisions and take action consistently over time that forwards the accumulation of money for the long-term.

ABOUT THE AUTHOR

Jackie Black, Ph.D., dubbed the Love and Relationship Doctor by Cosmo U.K., knows that "Love is never enough!"

Successful, committed couples need to develop emotional intelligence; learn, practice and master essential relationship success skills; and must be courageous, compassionate, committed, tolerant and persistent.

Dr. Jackie serves men and women who are serious, relationship-minded singles, pre-married, newly-married, new parents, long-time married; couples and families facing illness, and those grieving the death of a loved one.

Dr. Jackie is a popular Internet syndicated columnist, radio personality, and a veteran lecturer and educator. She delivers her monthly Relationship Tip Sheet to men and women in over 38 countries. Her high-content and fast-paced downloadable podcasts focus on current, and sometimes controversial, relationship-driven issues.

Dr. Jackie is a frequent guest expert on radio stations throughout the world and on Internet radio; and is regularly cited in major magazines in the U.S. and abroad.

Couples and Money: Cracking the code to ending the #1 conflict in marriage

Personal Coaching for Individuals and Couples by Telephone from Anywhere in the World

Dr. Jackie offers individualized support so you can learn and practice the essential relationship success skills detailed in this book. Your Relationship Coach is your personal trainer for your relationship! Working with a professional coach on a regular basis will move you through the stuck places much more quickly, and will provide an energized, creative and exciting place to learn, practice and master the essential, relationship success skills. Coaching will shorten your learning curve and will deepen and enliven your *attention* and *intention* to your Self, your partner and your relationship! Your Relationship Coach is your partner and champion supporting you to build or rebuild the life that you love with the love of your life!

For information about how to work with Dr. Jackie on the principles described in this book or on other relationship issues, please visit Dr. Jackie's web site at www.CrackingTheCodeBooks. com or email Dr. Jackie at DrJackie@CrackingTheCodeBooks. com.

Couples and Money Coaching Groups by Telephone from Anywhere in the World

Dr. Jackie's Couples and Money Coaching Groups are an opportunity to participate with several other couples in a group setting that is structured around cracking the code to ending the #1 conflict in marriage–issues related to money! Each person in the coaching group receives individual coaching from Dr. Jackie during every session, while at the same time benefits from the work, successes and challenges of the other group participants.

About The Author

A wonderful energy occurs when you come together in groups. Growth and change can be accelerated by the support and alliances between like-minded individuals. A sense of community is created by the group and for the group. It's a rich opportunity to give and receive the support and encouragement you need in your life to be your best and most brilliant Self. It is very powerful to talk about the deeply meaningful challenges you face in your life with others who are facing their own challenges.

For information about joining one of Dr. Jackie's Couples and Money coaching groups or coaching groups focused on other issues, please visit Dr. Jackie's web site at www. CrackingTheCodeBooks.com or email Dr. Jackie at DrJackie@ CrackingTheCodeBooks.com.

Couples and Money Train-The-Trainer by Telephone from Anywhere in the World

Dr. Jackie conducts a Couples and Money Train-The-Trainer Program for therapists, counselors, and certified and credentialed coaches who would like to work with their clients on the issues related to money and learning, practicing and mastering the essential relationship success skills required to do that.

For information about Dr. Jackie's Couples and Money Train-The-Trainer Program please email her at DrJackie@ CrackingTheCodeBooks.com

Dr Jackie's best-selling dating book, *Meeting Your Match: Cracking the code to successful relationships*, is the definitive guide that takes the reader through the process of meeting and dating in a straightforward and practical way. This book is a

175

Couples and Money: Cracking the code to ending the #1 conflict in marriage

treasure trove of information, all with step-by-step processes to take you from single to being part of a rewarding relationship– and isn't that what most of us really want?

Dr. Jackie's next books in the Cracking-the-Code series are *People Talking: Cracking the code to being understood,* and *Getting Older: Cracking the code to remembering when loved ones forget.* These books will be available in paperback and for your Kindle on Amazon.com soon.

A SNEAK PREVIEW OF
DR. JACKIE'S NEXT BOOK

PEOPLE TALKING

*Cracking the code
to being understood*

JACKIE BLACK, PHD

INTRODUCTION TO "PEOPLE TALKING"

People think that they know how to talk–they think that opening their mouths and speaking is actually communicating. It isn't!

Communication is really about being open; and when you are truly communicating you are vulnerable; and that is the only way you can help others really understand who you are and what you are saying. If you allow or invite someone to know you and to understand what you need and what you want, you will help them to understand what you can reasonably be expected to do and not do.

Real communication is about getting your needs met and meeting the needs of other people. It's as much about listening as talking.

When you are communicating honestly and openly you are insuring that both people in the relationship understand what the other is all about.

So why did I decide to write this book? Aren't there enough books on *effective communication* around?

Of course, there are many books about the theories and mechanics of communication, but after working with people in relationships who were struggling for such a long time, I realized that these books didn't get to the root of the problem. The thing that kept coming up was that people were not allowing themselves to be known. They would say things that weren't meaningful and authentic; abut who they really were. They were, effectively communicating with the brakes on.

179

Couples and Money: Cracking the code to ending the #1 conflict in marriage

So often when people talk they talk about the other person—what they think the other person is thinking, what they believe the other person is doing, what they fear the other person is feeling; all the time judging, and attributing behaviors to that poor *other* person, based on their own view of the world. When people talk about themselves, they are often constructing a façade that is a defence mechanism. The purpose of their communication is NOT about being known. In fact, people who talk about themselves all the time often find it the toughest to speak honestly and openly about themselves.

It's important that your 'I' is in your communication—so others understand what you want and need. It doesn't mean that you are self-absorbed, it is just helping the people with whom you have close relationships to know you more deeply and more easily. If you permit people to see you accurately then there is a much higher likelihood that you will be accurately understood.

The same applies when you are listening to the people with whom you have close relationships. If you can support them to communicate their real wants and needs you are laying the groundwork for a strong relationship that will run into far fewer problems.

I started writing this book for couples who are in committed relationships, but soon realized that communication is a life skill and it was quickly apparent that these communication skills apply in all areas of life. So communicating in business and in family relationships became important to include.

You can't be honest in some relationships and not others! Once the door is open, it is open! There is no going back or only opening it for certain people. Once you become more skilled and practiced

180

A Sneak Preview of Dr. Jackie's Next Book
People Talking: Cracking the code to being understood

at open, honest communication you'll find that your willingness to be known deeply and accurately by everybody will abound, and will make a profound difference in the quality of all your relationships, and the deepen and enrich the authentic connections with those with whom you are in relationship!

Treat this book as a tool to improve relationship in all areas–don't just read it–take action! Read, do the exercises, practice–it's not a theoretical exercise! You'll need to put some effort in.

When you've worked through the chapters–you'll get a new understanding of how communicating really works. You will learn, practice and master grounded, solid communication skills and your relationships will flourish at a whole new level!

Remember, only YOU can make it happen!

Jackie Black, Ph.D.
Southern California
USA

Chapter 1

RELATIONSHIPS–AND COMMUNICATION

In your life you'll experience many relationships, with your parents, partner, bosses, colleagues, people who work for you and friends, and all of them will flourish, flounder or fail–based on the communication within that relationship.

A baby can't talk, but can certainly make his needs known! Mothers learn to interpret the different types of cry and can usually tell the difference between "uncomfortable," "hungry" and "bored"! The communication medium may not be words, but the message is crystal clear.

Fathers don't always attain the same ability to interpret different cries. This is usually when they are not as closely involved with the day-to-day care of the baby. If a father is the main care-provider he will be able to interpret the cries and know whether his son or daughter needs a clean diaper, a bottle or simply some distraction.

So what does that tell us?

Perhaps that it takes proximity and close attention to understand each individual's method of communication.

With a baby you will make the effort because you know that the responsibility for their wellbeing depends on you. As we attain adulthood, we expect others to accommodate our method of communication. It often becomes a one way street with an expectation that other people should "take us as we are."

183

We unconsciously expect that the people who love us will accommodate our chosen approach to communication, simply because they do love us. The problems that arise in most relationships are directly related to a breakdown or mismatch in the way the people communicate. So why do we expect them to do it "our way"–and abdicate responsibility for ensuring that our communications are clear and accurate?

Also why should the people we meet in our workplace, or in our social activities, make allowances for our chosen style of communicating, if it doesn't suit them?

Our parents will expect us to learn their "rules" and will "teach" us their expectations for behavior, including communication. As we grow and develop other influences affect our behavior and method of communication; teachers, friends, children at school, adults with whom we spend a substantial amount of time.

Teachers can be a strong influence, but, often, the biggest influence on behavior of any child is that of the other children with whom they spend their time. Unless a child is schooled at home, this is most likely the children in their class and age group at school.

The 'Kevin' syndrome

In the UK there is a comedian called Harry Enfield who has created a character called Kevin. Kevin is a teenager – with a friend called Perry. Kevin's parents find communicating with Kevin completely beyond them! He grunts, says unintelligible words, gets angry for no reason and is generally difficult. Perry and Kevin seem to communicate with each other in this "teenage language" of grunts and strange words.

A Sneak Preview of Dr. Jackie's Next Book
People Talking: Cracking the code to being understood

However, a complete change takes place when Perry talks to Kevin's parents when he suddenly becomes polite and well-mannered. Similarly, Kevin communicates with Perry's mother in the same well-mannered way, whilst Perry still grunts and snarls at his parents.

This indicates that, whilst Kevin and Perry have developed their own means of communication that sets them apart from "grown-ups," they conform to expectations with adults outside their own family. The learned behavior to respect adults rises to the forefront.

It may seem to be a case of familiarity breeds contempt, but this is typical of most close relationships, where we expect those closest to us to make allowances and trust that they care about us enough to accept us as we choose to be.

Communicating is a behavior–and Kevin and Perry choose to be respectful to adults outside their own family. However, it's an unconscious behavior, and real life "Kevin's" may not realize they are being different.

What is authentic behavior?

I was presenting a seminar and one of the female delegates was acting up. She over-reacted to comments, made a commotion in group discussions and disrupted the whole session.

During a break I approached her. "I understand that you are expressing your feelings about what we are discussing, but you're making it difficult for everyone by expressing your feelings so vocally," I explained.

"I'm just being authentic, its how I feel and you are telling us we should not hide our feelings," she defended herself.

"If you were in your children's school, feeling all the things you're feeling now would you behave this way?" I asked her.

"Heaven's no," she said, looking shocked. "I thought I was expressing my feelings, isn't that what we are supposed to be doing?"

I explained, "Talking about your feelings is important, but that doesn't mean you have to be your feelings– and act them out. What I was talking about was finding the words that help people to understand our experiences."

This woman's misunderstanding is not uncommon–and many people don't realize that the way they behave is a direct result of the environment they've lived in, worked in and, most influential, brought up in.

The boss isn't always right!

When I worked in a large organization we had a new parking system introduced–with gates that needed a card to enter.

A Sneak Preview of Dr. Jackie's Next Book
People Talking: Cracking the code to being understood

One day soon after this had been installed the president came to me and asked for a new parking card. As president he had originally been issued with card number 001, but his wife's dog had chewed up his card.

I called the administrator only to be told that he could not have another card with the number 001. The security system only allowed one issue of each number.

The president was in a high level meeting, but called me in to find out if his card was ready. I leaned over and quietly explained that he could not have another card with 001 on it. He went crazy in the conference room, which was full of people and was connected to another room full of people on a conference call too. He shouted at me and was abusive.

I went out and walked around the block. I was in turmoil and felt demeaned by his attack. I won't tolerate someone yelling at me and decided that this was not acceptable.

I returned to the office and left a note on his desk saying this behavior was not acceptable to me. The result was that he didn't speak to me for weeks!

Then one day we met at the elevator. "So nobody can yell at you, huh?" he said.

"That's right," I responded.

Couples and Money: Cracking the code to ending the #1 conflict in marriage

"Meet me in my office in 15 minutes with a list of all the reasons why people can't yell at you," he said.

I went straight to my desk and wrote my list, then I looked at it and decided to split it into two—one list that were things that I felt were OK to tell my boss and one list that were deeply personal.

Included in the latter list was that my parents yelled at me a lot when I was growing up and I vowed I would never accept that from anyone again.

Fifteen minutes later I walked into his office. He invited me to sit down.

"So nobody yells at you? Tell me about that. Why did you decide that?" he asked.

I went through the "safe" list one at a time, and then he stopped me. "Let me tell you a story," he said. "I grew up in a poor area of Brooklyn in a family of seven. I learned when I wanted someone's attention I had to be really big and really loud or people wouldn't hear me."

This man was well over six feet tall and certainly not someone you'd overlook! I was touched by his story and I understood what yelling was for him.

My mother's intention was against me; my boss's intention was on his own behalf.

188

A Sneak Preview of Dr. Jackie's Next Book
People Talking: Cracking the code to being understood

I looked him in the eye and said "You can yell at me whenever you want. Now I understand what it means for you."

"No," he responded, "I will never yell at you again, now that I understand what yelling means to you, I'll never put you in that place again."

I'm not suggesting that people should be allowed to yell at others, it's not right to be disrespectful to employees. However, it's important to recognize that, when we are in communication with people and we feel they don't understand what we need or feel they are not hearing us, then sometimes our personal experiences transcend or overwhelm our normal "good" behavior.

This is not necessarily the case in stressful situations. You need a skill set to deal with your needs or wants are being challenged in some way. This book will help you to develop those skills so you have a fall back to help you. You'll build your own superstructure that you can overlay onto your usual system of reaction.

This means that when you are under pressure you'll be able to make better choices than to resort to name calling, shouting, swearing or other highly emotional and unproductive responses.

The Importance of Communication in Relationships

When you meet someone for the first time you will normally make an effort to be pleasant and polite. This is especially true if it is someone whom you perceive to have an impact on your life in the future. For instance:

- At a job interview, you are likely to not only dress to impress, but to be on your best behavior.
- When you meet someone to whom you are attracted in a social situation you will make an effort to appear at your best.
- In a new job you will try to make a good impression on your new work colleagues.
- When you are introduced to a group by a friend you will normally try to fit in and connect with the others in the group.

Communication is the key to all these relationships.

Relationships flounder when the communication doesn't work. This can be for all sorts of reasons. Let's look at some examples of what happens when people stop trying.

Sally and Duncan

Sally was extrovert and full of energy. She had been dating Duncan for several months and things had settled down into a routine. Duncan was a strong character, but quieter than Sally and not comfortable with revealing his feelings.

Sally felt that something was wrong between them because Duncan rarely paid her compliments or expressed his feelings. Knowing that Duncan resisted discussions that were emotionally based, she became withdrawn. Duncan realized something was wrong, but didn't feel comfortable starting a conversation about it.

A Sneak Preview of Dr. Jackie's Next Book
People Talking: Cracking the code to being understood

The relationship moved into a downward spiral and eventually they parted–which wasn't what either of them really wanted–but without open communication a relationship was impossible to maintain.

Lack of communication is often the culprit; and while it is important to tell people how you feel, you must think first and work out a way to say whatever you want to say from a place of being respectful and responsible, and staying in personal integrity.

Monica and Beverley

Beverley worked for Monica in the purchasing department. Beverley was ambitious and keen to advance, she asked for assignments and was frustrated when Monica kept her on what appeared to be a "tight leash."

Monica could see that Beverley was eager to move up, but was also wary of letting go of some of the responsibilities to the younger woman. She confined Beverley by not allowing her to make decisions without permission at every stage.

After six months Beverley came to Monica and asked "Am I doing something wrong?"

"No, you're doing fine."

"Why don't you trust me to make decisions?" countered Beverley.

"I do, but you're not ready yet," responded Monica.

Couples and Money: Cracking the code to ending the #1 conflict in marriage

This is the point where the conversation could have gone either way, but Beverley's frustration surfaced.

"I'm ready, but you can't bear to let someone else show that they can do the job as well as you can. There's no reason why I should not take on this responsibility."

Whilst this was close to the truth, Monica was now backed into a corner and had to make a decision quickly as to how to deal with this. As with most human beings, the knee-jerk reaction is to hit back when threatened and she snapped, "You don't know what you're talking about, you've only been here five minutes and you think you can take over. Your attitude needs some work and I won't tolerate you speaking to me, or to any of your other colleagues in this way. This conversation is over."

You can imagine the atmosphere that resulted from this exchange–and the effect on the quality of the relationship between the two women, not to mention the impact on the other people in the team.

Inappropriate communication can be equally damaging–and can have catastrophic results. You only have to think of the story of Peter and the Wolf, which brings us to the issue of repeated requests. Someone once described "nagging" as an often repeated request and many people have said, usually in frustration, "If you'd done it when I first asked I wouldn't have had to nag!"

The problem with repeating requests is that, after a while, the listener stops listening! Add to the repetition, a perception of a

192

A Sneak Preview of Dr. Jackie's Next Book
People Talking: Cracking the code to being understood

lack of knowledge in a certain area and you have a recipe for serious communication breakdown.

Tim and Flora

Tim was into cars and would talk about the inner workings of the internal combustion engine with his friends at length, followed the Formula 1 World Championship and any other event featuring petrol driven machines. Flora, his partner, could drive competently, but really wasn't interested in how the machine worked.

She came home one day and said to Tim "The car is making a funny noise."

"What sort of noise?" asked Tim.

"It's a sort of wheezy rattle," explained Flora.

"I'll take a look later," said Tim, thinking it didn't sound like anything serious.

A couple of days later Flora said "Have you looked at the car yet?"

"No, I haven't had time," said Tim, meaning to take a look soon.

The weekend came and went. On Sunday evening Flora reminded Tim about the car again. He got annoyed and accused her of nagging.

Couples and Money: Cracking the code to ending the #1 conflict in marriage

On Wednesday evening Flora got home from work and observed "The rattle is getting louder, I can hear it over the radio now." Tim didn't respond.

Flora mentioned the rattle several times over the following couple of weeks. Tim was irritated by her "needling" and stubbornly refused to take action.

Eventually, after about three weeks, the exhaust system came off and Flora spent a considerable amount of time waiting for a mechanic to come and get the car in order to put a new exhaust on it.

When she told Tim what had happened–he responded "If you hadn't nagged me so much I would have done it!"

So how could any of these situations have been resolved in a more positive way? As we explore communication you'll discover how to communicate more effectively and get positive results–and great relationships.

Communication Breakdown

We've all heard people refer to communication breakdown– usually as the reason for something going wrong. But have you ever stopped to think about what that really means?

- What causes communication breakdown?
- What can you do to avoid it happening?
- Do you communicate consciously?
- Do you think about whether the other person has understood

A Sneak Preview of Dr. Jackie's Next Book
People Talking: Cracking the code to being understood

what you've said–or simply assume they have?

Let's take a look at the communication process. There are four main elements:

1. The first is putting your idea into order, this means choosing the words, tone, style and structure of the message.

2. Next you need to select the means of sending the message. There are times when a spoken communication face-to-face is better than telephone or email, and times when the written word is more powerful than anything that you could say verbally.

3. The third part is how the message is received–when someone hears or reads what you have to say.

4. Finally there is the process of "decoding," in other words understanding the message completely and accurately. This includes all the tonal nuances (or lack of them, in the case of the written word), the accompanying signals or influences, including any preconceptions your receiver might have.

There is sometimes an additional element where the cycle closes as you receive feedback or a response to your original communication.

Most of your communication will be done verbally either face-to-face or on the telephone, but communication breakdown happens when something goes wrong in the cycle of communication both in spoken and written form.

The Communication Cycle

In every communication there is a sender and a receiver. The breakdown in communication occurs somewhere in between these two and to identify where this is happening you'll need to be aware of all the steps that make up the process.

When you start to speak you won't analyze every word you are going to say–however, sometimes, when the conversation is important, it's wise to give some thought to what you want to say–and the message you want the person listening (or reading) to get.

Step one

In the cycle in communication the first step is to clarify the idea you have before trying to communicate it to someone else. It saves communication breakdown happening at the start.

Look at the diagram below–you'll see how the whole cycle works.

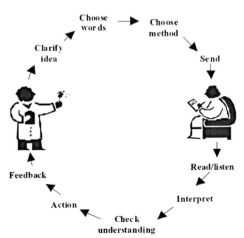

A Sneak Preview of Dr. Jackie's Next Book
People Talking: Cracking the code to being understood

So thinking about the idea you want to communicate before speaking may sound ridiculous, but how many times have you listened to someone who opens their mouth and says, "Er, you know what's-her-name, that blonde lady that use to work here, or did she? Well, she was on the floor below–at least I think she was. Anyway, she was here yesterday, or it might have been the day before, I think. Hang on, no, it was yesterday. Come to think of it she might not have been blonde when she worked here; I thought she looked different. She had a little girl with her, I don't remember her saying anything about children, but then I didn't talk to her that often ..."

This is known as engaging mouth without putting brain in gear! By the time this person has got to the point–if they ever had one–the listener has probably glazed over and stopped paying attention. The chances of any action or response occurring as a result of this kind of communication are negligible.

Mark and Jackie

My late husband, Mark, was going out to run a few errands for himself and I asked him to do 2 errands for me while he was out. "Could you stop at the dog food store and pick up food for Sophie and stop at the cleaners and collect my suit?" I asked.

"No problem," he said. I wrote a list with 1. Pick up dog food. 2. Go to cleaners for the suit–then drew a little heart and added a loving message. He went off with the list tucked in his pocket.

Couples and Money: Cracking the code to ending the #1 conflict in marriage

I must add that his errands would take him about 20 minutes away, the dry cleaner was closest to our house, and the dog food store was in the middle.

Some time later he returned and he was pretty frustrated.

"The dog food store closes at 1pm–why didn't you tell me? And by the time I'd gone back for the dog food, the cleaner had closed–I didn't know they closed at 2pm."

I'd written the list in the right order, but hadn't told Mark that there was a specific "to-do" order, and I hadn't given him any specific details about my errands. He hadn't followed the implicit instructions–because he didn't recognize the importance of the "order in which they were written." If I had communicated all of the details and the reason I had asked him to stop for dog food first then go to the cleaners, he would have said "Sure" and done the errands in that order based on the closing time of each business.

I was disappointed that I didn't get my suit out of the cleaners and that I had to make Sophie's food last through the weekend, and I also recognized that it was my responsibility to provide Mark the essential details and help him run my errands successfully.

198

A Sneak Preview of Dr. Jackie's Next Book
People Talking: Cracking the code to being understood

Step two

The second step is to choose the words you need to ensure your message is clear. That's not as silly as you might imagine. First, there is the issue of "jargon"–we all use it, whether it is related to the industry in which we work, the slang of our social group, or the "cool" language of the day.

We use abbreviations, short forms, and mnemonics in every day speech and frequently forget to check if the other person understands them all. In fact, we often assume they do understand– and then wonder why they don't respond as we expected.

Can you imagine two people discussing the WWF when one thinks they are talking about the World Wildlife Fund and the other is talking about the World Wrestling Federation?

If in doubt keep your message simple. People use long words or complex sentences and then wonder why others misunderstand them. If the information you provide is incorrect, inaccurate, confusing or complex, there will be problems with reception of the message. I was taught the KISS technique–keep it short and simple!

Step three

The third step in the process is to choose an appropriate method of sending your message.
- Do you think it is appropriate to invite your best friend to be your bridesmaid by email?
- How would you feel if your current partner ended the relationship by text message?
- Would a face-to-face chat be the right means of confirming

a contract with a supplier of services that cost a substantial amount?

- Would you ask your bank manager for a loan to set up a business by email?

Sometimes face-to-face is right, sometimes there needs to be something in writing. Sometimes a casual approach works perfectly, other times it's important to be more formal.

Step four–Getting the message

While it is the sender's responsibility to ensure that the information is correct, accurate, clear and in as simple form as possible, it is equally the receiver's responsibility to check that what they have understood is correct.

If you're on the receiving end of the communication then there are things you should do to ensure you get the message accurately. The first, and most important, is to listen (or read) carefully. Communication breakdown occurs as much on the receiving side as on the sending side.

People mishear and then take action–and frustration results all around for time wasted and actions taken at the wrong time, with the wrong person, with the wrong information.

Of course, sometimes things that we mishear can be very funny, but when you are trying to build a relationship, or maintain an existing relationship–miscommunication can be disastrous.

A Sneak Preview of Dr. Jackie's Next Book
People Talking: Cracking the code to being understood

Step five

Having heard or read the message the next part of the reception process is to interpret what has been said. This step is full of pitfalls! Ask any man who has been in a long term relationship with a woman! Unfortunately, women tend to communicate obliquely–in other words they don't always say exactly what they mean.

The shopping is in the car

It's a sunny day and Julia arrives home from the supermarket with a car full of shopping. Tom is watching the ball game on the TV and it's a good game.

Julia walks through the door and announces, "The shopping is in the car."

Tom grunts–and thinks "I'll get it during the break."

With no immediate sign of action Julia gets annoyed. "Fine, I'll get it myself," she says and stomps out to the car.

She then brings in the first batch with much sighing and muttering. Tom realizes that he has done something wrong (although he is not sure what) and abandons the game. "You could have left that for me to do," he says.

"And the frozen food would have been ruined by the time you got around to it," she snaps back.

Couples and Money: Cracking the code to ending the #1 conflict in marriage

"You didn't mention that," he objects.

"Why else would I have asked you to get it?"

Tom makes a mental note to check what Julia means in future–and wonders how soon he can get back to the game without her becoming even more upset!

Julia wonders why men are so lazy and have to be asked to do everything.

Men and women communicate in different ways–interpreting what is meant can be a real minefield. Even men and women who have been in a long term relationship forget that they have different means of getting their message across and are still surprised when there are misunderstandings.

This is not confined to communication between the genders; business communication can often be influenced by all sorts of things. For instance, some people will not put their real thoughts in writing, in case they upset someone with the power to make life uncomfortable. What they do instead is communicate by hints, references and omissions. In order to understand what they really mean you need a comprehensive knowledge of the person, their motivations and the situation in which they operate. This is a real situation of needing to read between the lines!

The political maneuverings of managers in any business are likely to be full of this kind of communication–making getting a clear message increasingly difficult.

A Sneak Preview of Dr. Jackie's Next Book
People Talking: Cracking the code to being understood

Step six

If you don't do this step you will be contributing to one of the most frequent causes of communication breakdown–and it's based on checking your information. Ask questions, clarify and repeat back what you have understood. The ultimate aim is to get the right information right the first time. It is the receiver's responsibility to check their understanding of the message is correct.

Be an active listener. Repeat what you have understood to be sure your understanding is what the sender is trying to convey. This doesn't mean repeating everything someone has said, but summarizing and questioning to ensure you are on track. This is particularly important if the message is long and complex.

Step seven

The last part of the cycle is to take action based on what has been said and provide feedback of some kind to reassure the person who started the communication that you heard (read), understood, and took action.

If you don't let people know what happened they may simply assume that you've either done what they expected–or worse, done nothing. Keeping people informed helps to strengthen your relationship.

Assumptions, preconceptions, premature conclusions are all dangerous activities. The golden rules are:

- Never assume anything, always check.

- Don't let preconceptions color your decision making - make sure you have all the facts.

203

Couples and Money: Cracking the code to ending the #1 conflict in marriage

- Don't jump to conclusions - make sure you KNOW. If you're not sure, then ask.

Before we go on

Review this chapter and think about what has "rung bells" for you.

Do you expect people to just get what you're saying when you're in "default style" or do you intentionally communicate so that you are known and heard accurately?

Do you communicate differently when you think that the risk is high—for instance, when it's important to make an impression or not to upset someone?

How often have you experienced communication breakdown?

What could you do to reduce the instances of communication breakdown?

Are you beginning to see the importance and value of intentional communication instead of reactive communication?

Think about one thing that you could do that would change your communication for the better—what would happen if you made that change?